The Observer's Pocket Series

AIRCRAFT

Observer's Books

NATURAL HISTORY
Birds · Birds' Eggs · Wild Animals · Zoo Animals
Farm Animals · Freshwater Fishes · Sea Fishes
Tropical Fishes · Butterflies · Larger Moths
Insects and Spiders · Pond Life · Sea and Seashore
Seashells · Dogs · Horses and Ponies · Cats · Trees
Wild Flowers · Grasses · Mushrooms · Lichens
Cacti · Garden Flowers · Flowering Shrubs
House Plants · Vegetables · Geology · Weather
Astronomy

SPORT
Association Football · Cricket · Golf · Coarse
Fishing · Fly Fishing · Show Jumping
Motor Sport

TRANSPORT
Automobiles · Aircraft · Commercial Vehicles
Motorcycles · Steam Locomotives · Ships · Small
Craft · Manned Spaceflight · Unmanned Spaceflight

ARCHITECTURE
Architecture · Churches · Cathedrals

COLLECTING
Awards and Medals · Coins · Postage Stamps
Glass · Pottery and Porcelain

ARTS AND CRAFTS
Music · Painting · Modern Art · Sculpture
Furniture · Sewing

HISTORY AND GENERAL INTEREST
Ancient Britain · Flags · Heraldry · European
Costume

TRAVEL
London · Tourist Atlas GB

The Observer's Book of

AIRCRAFT

COMPILED BY
WILLIAM GREEN

WITH SILHOUETTES BY
DENNIS PUNNETT

DESCRIBING 137 AIRCRAFT
WITH 245 ILLUSTRATIONS

1977 EDITION

FREDERICK WARNE

LIBRARY OF CONGRESS CATALOG CARD NO: 57 4425

ISBN 0 7232 1562 6

Printed in Great Britain

INTRODUCTION TO THE 1977 EDITION

With passing for press of this, the 26th annual edition of *The Observer's Book of Aircraft*, it is instructive to recall the aeronautical highlights of the past twelve months, for the year was unquestionably of some moment in aviation annals. It began with initiation of scheduled supersonic passenger-carrying services by Concorde, the satisfaction of the Anglo-French manufacturers with their success being tempered as the year progressed, however, by the failure of Concorde to gain acceptance by other airlines. Its Soviet counterpart, the Tu-144, meanwhile flew experimental freight services which were to be discontinued late in the year, having revealed problems which have delayed indefinitely the passenger operation of the Tupolev SST by Aeroflot. The year saw controversy over the capabilities of the *Backfire* variable-geometry bomber, with the Soviet Union claiming a manifestly obvious strategic weapon to be purely tactical in role, and although the formal production programme for its US equivalent, the Rockwell International B-1, was initiated towards the year's end, its future was still by no means assured.

During the course of 1976, the Panavia Tornado was ordered into production; deliveries began to the RAF of the first of the new-generation basic and advanced jet trainers, the Hawk, and the F-15 Eagle attained operational status—the first new fighter to join the USAF combat equipment inventory in a decade. Even longer than a decade had elapsed since the world's absolute speed record had been raised, when, in July, this coveted prize was gained by the Lockheed SR-71A, while a few months later, a low-altitude (100 ft/30 m) speed record was to be claimed by another Lockheed aircraft, a privately-owned F-104 Starfighter. But none of these events was destined to receive more worldwide publicity than did the defection to Japan of a Soviet pilot with a MiG-25 fighter.

The year's aeronautical débutantes were comparatively few, the most significant being the Boeing YC-14 and, barely more than a week before the year's end, the first Soviet airbus-type transport, the Il-86, although an unheralded newcomer was the Soviet naval VTOL fighter, subsequently dubbed *Forger*, which appeared aboard the carrier *Kiev* when it first left home waters. These and the less spectacular of the year's newcomers are to be found in the following pages, together with the latest production versions of established types and a variety of aircraft expected to make their début during this edition's year of currency, such as Hawker Siddeley's Coastguarder maritime patroller, new military trainers, including the CASA C.101, HAL HPT-32 and RFB Fantrainer, the Sea Harrier shipboard V/STOL fighter and the American Jet 400 Hustler business aircraft.

The *raison d'être* of *The Observer's Book of Aircraft* continues to be the presentation in compact form of basic reference to the new aircraft types and variants of existing types that have appeared during the twelve months preceding issue of this edition or may be expected to appear during the volume's year of currency.

WILLIAM GREEN

AERITALIA G.222

Country of Origin: Italy.

Type: General-purpose military transport.

Power Plant: Two 3,400 shp General Electric T64-P4D turboprops.

Performance: Max. speed, 329 mph (530 km/h) at sea level, 336 mph (540 km/h) at 15,000 ft (4 575 m); normal cruise, 224 mph (360 km/h) at 14,750 ft (4 500 m); range with 11,025-lb (5 000-kg) payload, 1,920 mls (3 250 km), with max. fuel, 3,262 mls (5 250 km); max. initial climb rate, 1,890 ft/min (9,6 m/sec).

Weights: Empty, 32,165 lb (14 590 kg); empty equipped, 33,950 lb (15 400 kg); max. take-off, 58,422 lb (26 500 kg).

Accommodation: Flight crew of three or four and seats for 44 fully-equipped troops or 40 paratroops. Alternative loads include 36 casualty stretchers, two jeep-type vehicles or equivalent freight.

Status: First and second prototypes flown July 18, 1970 and July 22, 1971, respectively, with first production aircraft flying on December 23, 1975. Italian Air Force has a requirement for 44 aircraft and had received three by the beginning of 1977. One ordered by Dubai (4th production) was delivered in October 1976, and two (8th and 9th production) of three ordered by Argentina were scheduled for delivery in January and February 1977 respectively. Production rate of two per month scheduled for March 1977.

Notes: Second prototype adapted for fire-fighting trials during summer of 1976.

AERITALIA G.222

Dimensions: Span, 94 ft 5¾ in (28,80 m); length, 74 ft 5½ in (22,70 m); height, 32 ft 1¾ in (9,80 m); wing area, 882·6 sq ft (82,00 m²).

AERMACCHI MB.339

Country of Origin: Italy.

Type: Two-seat basic and advanced trainer (and light tactical strike aircraft).

Power Plant: One 4,000 lb (1 814 kg) Fiat-built Rolls-Royce Viper Mk 632–43 turbojet.

Performance: Max. speed, 558 mph (898 km/h) at sea level or Mach 0·73, 508 mph (817 km/h) at 30,000 ft (9 145 m) or Mach 0·77; ferry range (10% reserves), 1,310 mls (2 110 km); initial climb, 7,000 ft/min (35,8 m/sec); service ceiling, 48,000 ft (14 630 m).

Weights: Empty equipped, 6,779 lb (3 075 kg); loaded (clean), 9,590 lb (4 350 kg); max. take-off (tactical strike), 12,996 lb (5 895 kg).

Armament: (Light strike) One 7,62-mm GAU-2B/A multi-barrel machine gun with 1,500 rounds or one 30-mm DEFA cannon with 120 rounds in flush-mounted ventral pod. Various stores on four 1,000-lb (453,5-kg) and two 750-lb (340-kg) capacity underwing pylons.

Status: First of two prototypes flown on August 12, 1976, with second scheduled to join test programme March 1977. Italian Air Force has a requirement for up to 100 with initial production deliveries for 1978.

Notes: The MB.339 is based on the airframe of late production versions of the MB.326 (see 1974 edition) and incorporates the strengthened wing and centre section of the single-seat MB.326K light strike aircraft, which, being optimised for low-level operation, provides a training role fatigue life of at least 10,000 hours. The armament pod (inserted in a bay beneath the rear seat) is interchangeable with photo-reconnaissance equipment.

AERMACCHI MB.339

Dimensions: Span (over tip tanks), 35 ft 7 in (10,85 m); length, 36 ft 0 in (10,97 m); height, 12 ft 10¼ in (3,92 m); wing area, 207·74 sq ft (19,30 m²).

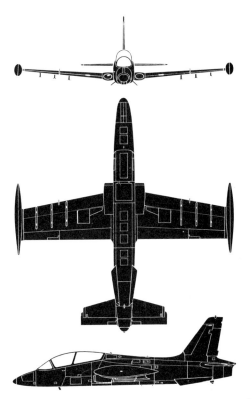

AIRBUS A300B4

Country of Origin: International consortium.
Type: Medium-haul commercial transport.
Power Plant: Two 51,000 lb (23 130 kg) General Electric CF6-50C turbofans.
Performance: Max. cruise, 586 mph (943 km/h) at 25,000 ft (7 620 m); econ. cruise, 554 mph (891 km/h) at 31,000 ft (9 450 m); long-range cruise, 585 mph (941 km/h) at 33,000 ft (10 060 m); range with max. payload, 2,530 mls (4 074 km); max. range (with 47,690-lb/21 633-kg payload), 4,014 mls (6 315 km).
Weights: Operational empty, 192,700 lb (87 409 kg); max. take-off, 330,700 lb (150 000 kg).
Accommodation: Flight crew of three and various arrangements for 220–300 passengers, or high-density arrangement for 345 passengers in nine-abreast seating.
Status: First and second A300Bs (dimensionally to B1 standard) flown October 28, 1972, and February 5, 1973, respectively, with third A300B (to B2 standard) flying on June 28, 1973. First A300B to B4 standard flown December 26, 1974. Orders and options for 56 placed by beginning of 1977 when production was running at 22 per annum.
Notes: The A300B is manufactured by a consortium comprising Aérospatiale (France), Deutsche Airbus (Federal Germany), Hawker Siddeley (UK) and Fokker-VFW (Netherlands). The first and second aircraft (A300B1s) had a 167 ft 2¼ in (50,97 m) fuselage, and the current B2 and B4 are dimensionally similar to each other, the latter having increased weights and fuel capacity, and wing leading-edge Krueger flaps to improve take-off performance.

AIRBUS A300B4

Dimensions: Span, 147 ft 1¼ in (44,84 m); length, 175 ft 11 in (53,62 m); height, 54 ft 2 in (16,53 m); wing area, 2,799 sq ft (260,0 m²).

AMERICAN JET 400 HUSTLER

Country of Origin: USA.
Type: Light business executive transport.
Power Plant: One 850 shp Pratt & Whitney (Canada) PT6A-41 turboprop and one 660 lb (299 kg) Teledyne CAE J402-CA-700 turbojet (for standby power).
Performance: (Estimated for turboprop only) Max. cruise, 380 mph (611 km/h) at 20,000 ft (6 095 m); econ. cruise, 330 mph (531 km/h) at 35,000 ft (10 670 m); range (with 30 min reserves) at max. cruise, 2,076 mls (3 340 km) at 20,000 ft (6 095 m), at econ. cruise, 2,970 mls (4 780 km); service ceiling, 36,200 ft (11 035 m).
Weights: (Estimated) Empty, 3,700 lb (1 678 kg); max. take-off, 6,500 lb (2 948 kg).
Accommodation: Pilot and co-pilot/passenger on flight deck and five passengers in main cabin with central aisle.
Status: First of three prototypes (built on production tooling) was scheduled to commence its test programme in late December 1976, with production deliveries projected for second half of 1977.
Notes: The Hustler utilises a small tail-mounted turbojet to boost take-off and climb performance from small airfields. The wing is of supercritical design and has full-span Fowler flaps, and lateral control is provided by two spoilers on each outer wing section. The Hustler is being certificated as a single-engined aircraft.

AMERICAN JET 400 HUSTLER

Dimensions: Span, 32 ft 7½ in (9,95 m); length, 38 ft 5 in (11,71 m); height, 10 ft 9 in (3,28 m); wing area, 181·15 sq ft (16,83 m²).

ANTONOV AN-30 (CLANK)

Country of Origin: USSR.

Type: Aerial survey aircraft.

Power Plant: Two 2,820 ehp Ivchenko AI-24T turboprops and one 1,764 lb (800 kg) Tumansky RU-19A-300 auxiliary turbojet.

Performance: Max. speed, 323 mph (520 km/h) at 19,685 ft (6 000 m); normal cruise, 264 mph (425 km/h); initial climb, 1,575 ft/min (8,0 m/sec); service ceiling, 27,230 ft (8 300 m); range, 1,616 mls (2 600 km); endurance, 6 hrs.

Weights: Empty equipped, 32,408 lb (14 700 kg); max. take-off, 50,706 lb (23 000 kg).

Accommodation: Standard crew of seven, including pilot, co-pilot, navigator, engineer and three photographers/ systems operators.

Status: The prototype An-30 initiated its flight test programme mid-1973 and the production model entered service with Aeroflot during the course of 1975.

Notes: The An-30 is a specialised aerial survey derivative of the An-24RT which, in turn, is a specialised freighter version of the An-24V *Seriiny II* (see 1969 edition) commercial transport. For the primary task of aerial photography for mapmaking, the An-30 is provided with four large survey cameras, and hatches permit the use of laser, thermographic, gravimetric, magnetic and geophysical sensors. The An-30 may also be used for microwave radiometer survey or mineral prospecting. Equipment includes a computer into which is fed a pre-programmed flight path, the computer subsequently controlling aircraft speed, altitude and course throughout the mission.

ANTONOV AN-30 (CLANK)

Dimensions: Span, 95 ft $9\frac{1}{2}$ in (29,20 m); length, 79 ft $7\frac{1}{8}$ in (24,26 m); height, 27 ft $3\frac{1}{2}$ in (8,32 m); wing area, 807·1 sq ft (74,98 m²).

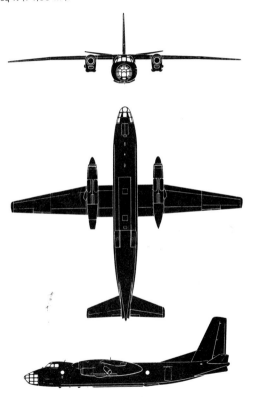

BAC ONE-ELEVEN 475

Country of Origin: United Kingdom.

Type: Short- to medium-range commercial transport.

Power Plant: Two 12,550 lb (5 692 kg) Rolls-Royce Spey 512-14-DW turbofans.

Performance: Max. cruise, 548 mph (882 km/h) at 21,000 ft (6 400 m); econ. cruise, 507 mph (815 km/h) at 25,000 ft (7 620 m); range with reserves for 230 mls (370 km) diversion and 45 min, 2,095 mls (3 370 km), with capacity payload, 1,590 mls (2 560 km).

Weights: Basic operational, 51,814 lb (23 502 kg); max. take-off, 92,000 lb (41 730 kg).

Accommodation: Basic flight crew of two and up to 89 passengers. Typical arrangement provides for 16 first- (four-abreast) and 49 tourist-class (five-abreast) passengers.

Status: Aerodynamic prototype of One-Eleven 475 flown August 27, 1970 followed by first production model on April 5, 1971, with certification and first production deliveries following in June. Total of 222 examples of all versions of the One-Eleven ordered by beginning of 1977.

Notes: The One-Eleven 475 combines the standard fuselage of the Series 400 with the redesigned wing and uprated engines of the Series 500 (see 1970 edition), coupling these with a low-pressure undercarriage to permit operation from gravel or low-strength sealed runways. The One-Eleven prototype flew on August 20, 1963, production models including the physically similar Series 200 and 300 with 10,330 lb (4 686 kg) Spey 506s and 11,400 lb (5 170 kg) Spey 511s, the Series 400 modified for US operation, and the Series 500 which is similar to the 475 apart from the fuselage and undercarriage. A passenger/cargo version of the 475 for the Sultan of Oman's Air Force is illustrated.

16

BAC ONE-ELEVEN 475

Dimensions: Span, 93 ft 6 in (28,50 m); length, 93 ft 6 in (28,50 m); height, 24 ft 6 in (7,47 m); wing area, 1,031 sq ft (95,78 m²).

BAC-AÉROSPATIALE CONCORDE

Countries of Origin: United Kingdom and France.
Type: Long-range supersonic commercial transport.
Power Plant: Four 38,050 lb (17 259 kg) reheat Rolls-Royce/SNECMA Olympus 593 Mk. 602 turbojets.
Performance: Max. cruise, 1,354 mph (2179 km/h) at 51,300 ft (15 635 m) or Mach 2·05; range with max. fuel (22,250-lb/10 092-kg payload and FAR reserves), 3,915 mls (6 300 km), with max. payload (28,000 lb/12 700 kg) at Mach 0·93 at 30,000 ft (9 145 m), 3,063 mls (4 930 km), at Mach 2·05, 3,869 mls (6 226 km); initial climb rate, 5,000 ft/min (25,4 m/sec); service ceiling (approx.), 60,000 ft (18 300 m).
Weights: Operational empty, 174,750 lb (79 265 kg); max. take-off, 400,000 lb (181 435 kg).
Accommodation: Normal flight crew of three and one-class seating for 128 passengers. Alternative high-density arrangement for 144 passengers.
Status: First and second prototypes flown March 2 and April 9, 1969, respectively. First of two pre-production aircraft flew December 17, 1971, and the first production example following on December 6, 1973, this having been joined by nine others by 1977 when six Concordes were under construction.
Notes: The Concorde began to operate its first fare-paying passengers in January 1976, services being initiated simultaneously by British Airways and Air France, these airlines having five and four Concordes on order respectively. Preliminary purchase agreements have been signed by China's CAAC (three) and Iran Air (two plus one on option).

BAC-AÉROSPATIALE CONCORDE

Dimensions: Span, 83 ft 10 in (25,56 m); length, 202 ft 3$\frac{3}{5}$ in (61,66 m); height, 37 ft 1 in (11,30 m); wing area, 3,856 sq ft (358,25 m²).

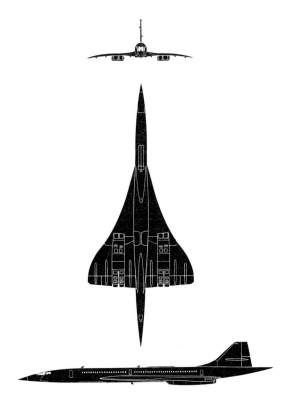

BEECHCRAFT MODEL 76

Country of Origin: USA.
Type: Light cabin monoplane.
Power Plant: Two 180 hp Avco Lycoming 0-360 series six-cylinder horizontally-opposed engines.
Performance: Max. cruise speed, 185 mph (298 km/h); range (with 45 min reserves), in excess of 800 mls (1 290 km).
Weights: No details available for publication.
Accommodation: Four seats in pairs with dual controls as standard and provision for up to 180 lb (81,6 kg) of baggage in separate compartment.
Status: Prototype flown late summer of 1974 as PD (Preliminary Design) 289 and decision to launch production taken in autumn of 1975 with first customer deliveries scheduled for autumn of 1977.
Notes: Closely related to the single-engined Sierra 200 and utilising some common structural components, the Model 76 is being manufactured with a honeycomb-bonded wing and by comparison with the prototype illustrated above has electrically- in place of manually-operated flaps, electrically-operated trim tabs and a new oleo undercarriage shock-absorbing system. Like the Model 77 (see pages 22–23), the Model 76 has been designed as a low-cost, high-volume-production aircraft and is to be marketed through the Beech Aero Centers at which it is expected to become the primary twin trainer.

BEECHCRAFT MODEL 76

Dimensions: Span, 38 ft 0 in (11,59 m); length, 29 ft 0 in (8,84 m); height, 8 ft 11 in (2,71 m).

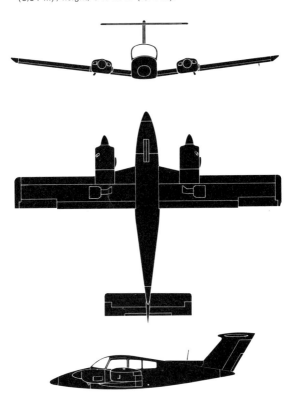

BEECHCRAFT MODEL 77

Country of Origin: USA.

Type: Side-by-side two-seat primary trainer.

Power Plant: One 115 hp Avco Lycoming 0-235-C1B four-cylinder horizontally-opposed engine.

Performance: No details available for publication at the time of closing for press.

Weights: Max. take-off, 1,650 lb (748 kg).

Status: Prototype of the Model 77 flown as the PD 285 on February 6, 1975, initial trials being conducted with a 100 hp Continental 0-200 engine and a low-set tailplane. During the course of subsequent development, a 115 hp Avco Lycoming 0-235 engine was adopted and the tail surfaces were redesigned, the horizontal surfaces being repositioned at the tip of the vertical surfaces. A decision to initiate production was taken during 1976, with first deliveries scheduled for 1978.

Notes: The Model 77 primary trainer has been evolved as a low-cost, high-volume-production aircraft which it is intended to incorporate in the Beech Aero Center flight student programmes. It employs advanced technology, including the new NASA-developed GAW-1 high-lift aerofoil section which is an outgrowth of high-speed supercritical aerofoil technology. A ventral tunnel houses primary flight controls and aluminium honeycomb is used in the construction.

BEECHCRAFT MODEL 77

Dimensions: Span, 30 ft 0 in (9,14 m); length, 23 ft 10¾ in (7,28 m); height, 7 ft 6½ in (2,30 m).

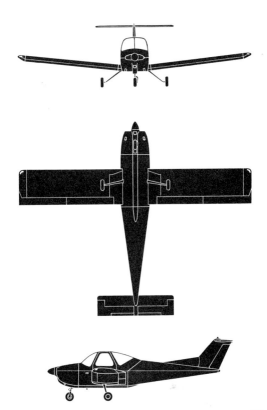

BEECHCRAFT SUPER KING AIR 200

Country of Origin: USA.

Type: Light business executive transport.

Power Plant: Two 850 shp Pratt & Whitney (Canada) PT6A-41 turboprops.

Performance: Max. cruise, 333 mph (536 km/h) at 12,000 ft (3 655 m), 320 mph (515 km/h) at 25,000 ft (7 620 m); max. range, 1,840 mls (2 961 km) at 27,000 ft (8 230 m) at max. cruise, 2,172 mls (3 495 km) at max. range cruise; initial climb, 2,450 ft/min (12,44 m/sec); service ceiling, 32,300 ft (9 845 m).

Weights: Empty equipped, 7,650 lb (3 470 kg); max. take-off, 12,500 lb (5 670 kg).

Accommodation: Flight crew of two and standard arrangement of six individual seats in main cabin with an optional eight-passenger arrangement. High-density configuration available for up to 13 passengers.

Status: Prototype Super King Air flown October 27, 1972, with second example following on December 15. Customer deliveries commenced March 1974, with some 250 delivered by beginning of 1977.

Notes: The Super King Air 200 is the fourth aircraft in the King Air range and differs from the King Air B100 (see 1976 edition) primarily in having increased wing span and a T-tail arrangement. Thirty (with 750 hp PT6A-38s) are being delivered to the USAF as C-12As and 40 to the US Army as RU-21J Hurons.

BEECHCRAFT SUPER KING AIR 200

Dimensions: Span, 54 ft 6 in (16,60 m); length, 43 ft 9 in (13,16 m); height, 14 ft 11½ in (4,54 m); wing area, 303 sq ft (28,1 m²).

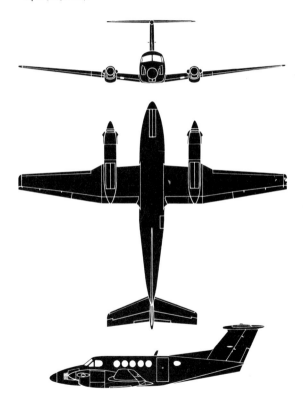

BEECHCRAFT T-34C TURBO MENTOR

Country of Origin: USA.
Type: Tandem two-seat primary trainer.
Power Plant: One 715 shp (derated to 400 shp) Pratt & Whitney (Canada) PT6A-45 turboprop.
Performance: Max. speed, 403 mph (649 km/h) at sea level; max. cruise, 213 mph (343 km/h) at sea level, 239 mph (384 km/h) at 10,000 ft (3 050 m); initial climb, 1,430 ft/min (7,27 m/sec); range (5% and 20 min reserves), 787 mls (1 265 km) at 220 mph (354 km/h) at 17,500 ft (5 340 m), 915 mls (1 470 km) at 222 mph (357 km/h) at 25,000 ft (7 625 m).
Weights: Approx empty, 2,940 lb (1 335 kg); max. take-off, 4,300 lb (1 952 kg).
Status: First of two YT-34Cs (converted from T-34Bs) flown on September 21, 1974, and 149 funded up to and including Fiscal Year 1977 Budget against anticipated US Navy requirement of 400 aircraft. Export orders placed by beginning of 1977 include 12 for Morocco and 14 for Ecuador.
Notes: The T-34C is an updated derivative of the original Model 45 primary trainer, a turboprop replacing the Continental O-470-13 horizontally-opposed piston engine. The PT6A-45 turboprop of the T-34C is fitted with a torque limiter to restrict output and thus ensure long engine life and constant performance over a wide range of temperatures and altitudes. An armament training version, the T-34C-1, is to commence testing mid-1977.

BEECHCRAFT T-34C TURBO MENTOR

Dimensions: Span, 33 ft 4 in (10,17 m); length, 28 ft 8½ in (8,75 m); height, 9 ft 10 in (3,00 m); wing area, 179·9 sq ft (16,71 m²).

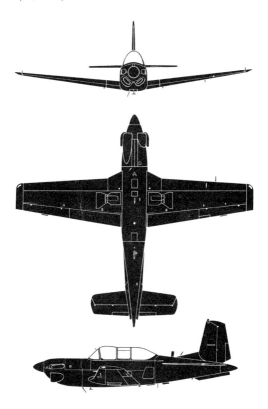

BELL (MODEL 301) XV-15

Country of Origin: USA.

Type: Two-seat tilt-rotor research aircraft.

Power Plant: Two 1,550 shp Avco Lycoming LTC1K-4K turboshafts.

Performance: (Estimated at 13,000 lb/897 kg) Max. speed, 389 mph (626 km/h); max. cruise, 360 mph (579 km/h); acceleration, 28 sec from hover to 276 mph (444 km/h); range (with reserves), 472 mls (760 km); endurance, 2·2 hrs.

Weights: Max. take-off (VTOL), 13,000 lb (5 897 kg); max. take-off (STOL), 15,000 lb (6 804 kg).

Status: First of two examples rolled out on October 22, 1976 with second scheduled to follow in February 1977. Flight testing scheduled to commence mid-1977.

Notes: The XV-15 is intended to prove the concept of tilt-rotor technology and is basically a conventional fixed-wing aircraft, but the wingtip-mounted engines and rotors may be swivelled to a vertical position for VTOL operations, then being progressively tilted to the horizontal for the high-speed forward flight mode, transition from vertical flight to high-speed forward flight and vice versa occupying approximately 12 seconds. The transmissions of the two turboshafts are interconnected to permit operation on a single engine and the aircraft is designed to attain a speed of 419 mph (674 km/h). US Army evaluation will include operational-type flight testing to study the application of the XV-15 concept in the reconnaissance and rescue roles.

BELL (MODEL 301) XV-15

Dimensions: Span (including engine nacelles), 35 ft 2 in (10,72 m); length, 42 ft 1 in (12,82 m); height (engines vertical), 15 ft 4 in (4,67 m).

BOEING MODEL 707-320C

Country of Origin: USA.

Type: Medium- to long-haul commercial transport.

Power Plant: Four 19,000 lb (8 618 kg) Pratt & Whitney JT3D-7 turbofans.

Performance: Max. cruise, 593 mph (956 km/h) at 30,000 ft (9 145 m); econ. cruise, 550 mph (885 km/h) at 35,000 ft (10 670 m); long-range cruise, 532 mph (856 km/h); range (max. payload of 84,000 lb/38 100 kg and no reserves), 4,300 mls (6 920 km), (max. fuel and no reserves), 7,475 mls (12 030 km).

Weights: Operational empty (passenger), 146,000 lb (66 224 kg), (cargo), 138,610 lb (62 872 kg); max. take-off, 333,600 lb (151 315 kg).

Accommodation: Max. accommodation for 219 economy-class passengers, but typical arrangement has 14 first-class and 133 coach-class seats.

Status: The prototype Model 707 first flew on July 15, 1954, the first production aircraft following on December 20, 1957. Production in a variety of versions has since continued and was running at one per month at the beginning of 1977, when sales of the Model 707 (and the Model 720 derivative) exceeded 920 and only the 707-320C was being offered.

Notes: The Model 707-320C has been sold in larger numbers than any version of the basic design, more than 330 having been delivered or being on order at the beginning of 1977. It is offered in convertible (cargo or mixed cargo–passenger) or all-cargo form, the latter having passenger facilities eliminated.

BOEING MODEL 707-320C

Dimensions: Span, 145 ft 9 in (44,42 m); length, 152 ft 11 in (46,61 m); height, 42 ft 5 in (12,93 m); wing area, 3,050 sq ft (283,4 m²).

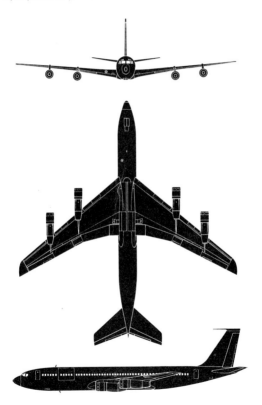

BOEING MODEL 727-200

Country of Origin: USA.

Type: Short- to medium-range commercial transport.

Power Plant: Three 14,500 lb (6 577 kg) Pratt & Whitney JT8D-9 turbofans (with 15,000 lb/6 804 kg JT8D-11s or 15,500 lb/7 030 kg JT8D-15s as options).

Performance: Max. speed, 621 mph (999 km/h) at 20,500 ft (6 250 m); max. cruise, 599 mph (964 km/h) at 24,700 ft (7 530 m); econ. cruise, 570 mph (917 km/h) at 30,000 ft (9 145 m); range with 26,400-lb (11 974-kg) payload and normal reserves, 2,850 mls (4 585 km), with max. payload (41,000 lb/18 597 kg), 1,845 mls (2 970 km).

Weights: Operational empty (basic), 97,525 lb (44 235 kg), (typical), 99,000 lb (44 905 kg); max. take-off, 208,000 lb (94 347 kg).

Accommodation: Crew of three on flight deck and six-abreast seating for 163 passengers in basic arrangement with max. seating for 189 passengers.

Status: First Model 727-100 flown February 9, 1963, with first delivery (to United) following October 29, 1963. Model 727-200 flown July 27, 1967, with first delivery (to Northeast) on December 11, 1967. Deliveries from mid-1972 have been of the so-called "Advanced 727-200" (to which specification refers and illustrations apply) and a total of 1,357 Model 727s had been ordered by the beginning of 1977 when some 1,220 had been delivered.

Notes: The Model 727-200 is a "stretched" version of the 727-100 (see 1972 edition). Deliveries of the "Advanced 727" with JT8D-17 engines of 16,000 lb (7 257 kg), permitting an increase of 3,500 lb (1 587 kg) in payload, began (to Mexicana) in June 1974. The proposed Model 727-300 with a 15-ft (4,57-m) longer fuselage, modified wing with Krueger flaps and extended wingtips, and a gross weight in excess of 210,000 lb (95 255 kg), was indefinitely shelved during 1975.

BOEING MODEL 727-200

Dimensions: Span, 108 ft 0 in (32,92 m); length, 153 ft 2 in (46,69 m); height, 34 ft 0 in (10,36 m); wing area, 1,700 sq ft (157,9 m²).

BOEING MODEL 737-200

Country of Origin: USA.

Type: Short-haul commercial transport.

Power Plant: Two 14,500 lb (6 577 kg) Pratt & Whitney JT8D-9 turbofans.

Performance: Max. speed, 586 mph (943 km/h) at 23,500 ft (7 165 m); max. cruise (at 90,000 lb/40 823 kg), 576 mph (927 km/h) at 22,600 ft (6 890 m); econ. cruise, 553 mph (890 km/h) at 30,000 ft (9 145 m); range (max. fuel and reserves), 2,530 mls (4 075 km), (max. payload of 34,790 lb/ 15 780 kg and reserves), 2,370 mls (3 815 km).

Weights: Operational empty, 60,210 lb (27 310 kg); max. take-off, 115,500 lb (52 390 kg).

Accommodation: Flight crew of two and up to 130 passengers in six-abreast seating with alternative arrangement for 115 passengers.

Status: Model 737 initially flown on April 9, 1967, with first deliveries (737-100 to Lufthansa) same year. Stretched 737-200 flown on August 8, 1967, with deliveries (to United) in 1968. Total sales amounted to 496 (including 19 -200s delivered to USAF as T-43A navigational trainers—see 1975 edition) by the beginning of 1977 when 470 had been delivered.

Notes: All aircraft delivered since May 1971 have been completed to the so-called "Advanced 737-200/C/QC" standard embodying improvements in range and short-field performance. A further stretched version, the 737-300, has been studied, but no decision to proceed with this has been taken.

BOEING MODEL 737-200

Dimensions: Span, 93 ft 0 in (28,35 m); length, 100 ft 0 in (30,48 m); height, 37 ft 0 in (11,28 m); wing area, 980 sq ft (91,05 m²).

BOEING MODEL 747-200B

Country of Origin: USA.

Type: Long-range large-capacity commercial transport.

Power Plant: Four 47,000 lb (21 320 kg) Pratt & Whitney JT9D-7W turbofans.

Performance: Max. speed at 600,000 lb (272 155 kg), 608 mph (978 km/h) at 30,000 ft (9 150 m); long-range cruise, 589 mph (948 km/h) at 35,000 ft (10 670 m); range with max. fuel and FAR reserves, 7,080 mls (11 395 km), with 79,618-lb (36 114-kg) payload, 6,620 mls (10 650 km); cruise ceiling, 45,000 ft (13 715 m).

Weights: Operational empty, 361,216 lb (163 844 kg); max. take-off, 775,000 lb (351 540 kg).

Accommodation: Normal flight crew of three and basic accommodation for 66 first-class and 308 economy-class passengers. Alternative layouts for 447 or 490 economy-class passengers nine- and 10-abreast respectively.

Status: First Model 747-100 flown on February 9, 1969, and first commercial services (by Pan American) inaugurated January 22, 1970. The first Model 747-200 (747B), the 88th aircraft off the assembly line, flown October 11, 1970. A total of 315 of all versions had been ordered by the beginning of 1977.

Notes: Principal versions are the -100 and -200 series, the latter having greater fuel capacity and increased maximum take-off weight, convertible passenger/cargo and all-cargo versions of the -200 series being designated 747-200C and 747-200F. The first production example of the latter flew on November 30, 1971. Deliveries of the Model 747SR, a short-range version of the 747-100 (to Japan Air Lines), began September 1973. The 747-200B was flown on June 26, 1973 with 51,000 lb (23 133 kg) General Electric CF6-50D engines, and the 52,500 lb (23 810 kg) CF6-50E and the 52,000 lb (23 585 kg) Rolls-Royce RB.211-524 are offered as optional installations.

BOEING MODEL 747-200B

Dimensions: Span, 195 ft 8 in (59,64 m); length, 231 ft 4 in (70,51 m); height, 63 ft 5 in (19,33 m); wing area, 5,685 sq ft (528,15 m²).

BOEING MODEL 747SP

Country of Origin: USA.

Type: Long-haul commercial transport.

Power Plant: Four 46,950 lb (21 296 kg) Pratt & Whitney JT9D-7A turbofans.

Performance: Max. cruise, 594 mph (957 km/h) at 35,000 ft (10 670 m); econ. cruise, 570 mph (918 km/h) at 35,000 ft (10 670 m); long-range cruise, 555 mph (893 km/h); range (with max. payload of 97,080 lb/44 034 kg), 6,620 mls (10 650 km), (with max. fuel and 30,000-lb/13 608-kg payload), 9,570 mls (15 400 km).

Weights: Operational empty, 315,000 lb (140 878 kg); max. take-off, 660,000 lb (299 370 kg).

Accommodation: Flight crew of three and basic accommodation for 28 first-class and 288 economy-class passengers. Max. high-density arrangement for 360 passengers in 10-abreast seating.

Status: First production Model 747SP flown July 4, 1975, with first customer deliveries (to Pan Am) following early 1976. Eighteen ordered by beginning of 1977.

Notes: The SP (Special Performance) version of the Model 747 embodies a reduction in overall length of 47 ft 7 in (14,30 m) and retains a 90% commonality of components with the standard Model 747 (see pages 36–37). The Model 747SP is intended primarily for operation over long-range routes where traffic densities are insufficient to support the standard model. Apart from having a shorter fuselage, the Model 747SP has taller vertical tail surfaces with a double-hinged rudder and new trailing-edge flaps.

BOEING MODEL 747SP

Dimensions: Span, 195 ft 8 in (59,64 m); length, 184 ft 9 in (56,31 m); height, 65 ft 5 in (19,94 m); wing area, 5,685 sq ft (528,15 m²).

BOEING E-3A

Country of Origin: USA.

Type: Airborne warning and control system aircraft.

Power Plant: Four 21,000 lb (9 525 kg) Pratt & Whitney TF33-PW-100/100A turbofans.

Performance: No details have been released for publication, but max. and econ. cruise speeds are likely to be generally similar to those of the equivalent commercial Model 707-320B (i.e., 627 mph/1 010 km/h and 550 mph/886 km/h respectively). Mission requirement is for 7-hr search at 29,000 ft (8 840 m) at 1,150 mls (1 850 km) from base. Unrefuelled endurance, 11·5 hrs.

Weights: Approx. max. take-off, 330,000 lb (149 685 kg).

Accommodation: The E-3A will carry an operational crew of 17 which may be increased according to mission. The complement comprises a flight crew of four, a four-man systems maintenance team, a battle commander and an eight-man air defence operations team.

Status: First of two EC-137D development aircraft flown February 9, 1972. Three pre-production examples of the operational derivative, the E-3A (one using EC-137D airframe), were produced, with the first (the EC-137D conversion) having commenced its trials in February 1975, and the second following in July 1975. Deliveries commenced in 1976 against initial contracts for 10 E-3As, total USAF requirement being 34 aircraft.

Notes: As part of a programme for the development of a new AWACS (Airborne Warning And Control System) aircraft for operation by the USAF from the mid 'seventies, two Boeing 707-320B transports were modified as EC-137D test-beds.

BOEING E-3A

Dimensions: Span, 145 ft 9 in (44,42 m); length, 152 ft 11 in (46,61 m); height, 42 ft 5 in (12,93 m); wing area, 3,050 sq ft (283,4 m²).

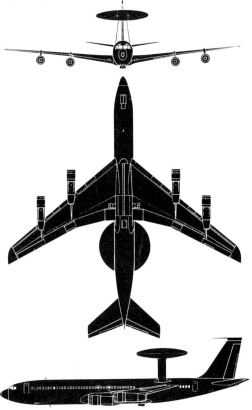

BOEING YC-14

Country of Origin: USA.

Type: Medium STOL tactical transport.

Power Plant: Two 51,000 lb (23 154 kg) General Electric YF103-GE-100 turbofans.

Performance: Max. speed, 518 mph (834 km/h) at 30,000 ft (9 150 m); typical cruise, 460 mph (740 km/h); mission radius (STOL operation and 27,000 lb/12 247 kg payload), 460 mls (740 km); range (conventional operation and 81,000 lb/36 740 kg payload), 1,150 mls (1 850 km); ferry range, 3,000 mls (4 827 km).

Weights: Operational empty, 124,000 lb (56 246 kg); max. take-off (STOL), 169,500 lb (76 880 kg), (conventional), 249,000 lb (112 945 kg); projected max. take-off, 300,000 lb (136 200 kg).

Accommodation: Flight crew of three and up to 150 troops or six cargo pallets plus 40 troops.

Status: Two prototypes flown August 9 and October 21, 1976. The YC-14 is competing with the McDonnell Douglas YC-15 (see pages 146–147) for USAF orders as an AMST (Advanced Military STOL Transport), current planning calling for the acquisition of a total of 277 AMSTs with service introduction commencing 1983.

Notes: The YC-14 is an advanced-technology transport utilising a supercritical wing with full-span variable-camber leading-edge flaps, boundary layer control and USB (Upper Surface Blowing) to achieve a combination of high speed performance and STOL (Short Take-Off and Landing) performance. USB is provided by engine exhaust gases flowing over the upper wing surfaces.

BOEING YC-14

Dimensions: Span, 129 ft 0 in (39,32 m); length, 131 ft 8 in (40,13 m); height, 48 ft 2 in (14,68 m); wing area, 1,762 sq ft (163,7 m²).

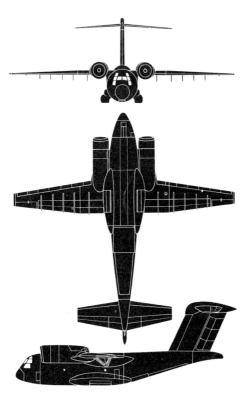

BRITTEN-NORMAN BN-2A-8S ISLANDER

Country of Origin: United Kingdom.
Type: Light utility transport.
Power Plant: Two 260 hp Avco Lycoming 0-540-E4C5 six-cylinder horizontally-opposed engines.
Performance: Max. speed, 170 mph (273 km/h) at sea level; cruise at 75% power, 160 mph (257 km/h) at 7,000 ft (2 140 m), at 67% power, 158 mph (253 km/h) at 9,000 ft (2 750 m), at 59% power, 154 mph (248 km/h) at 13,000 ft (3 960 m); range with standard fuel, 717 mls (1 154 km) at 160 mph (257 km/h), 870 mls (1 400 km) at 154 mph (248 km/h), tip tanks, 1,040 mls (1 674 km) at 160 mph (257 km/h), 1,263 mls (2 035 km) at 154 mph (248 km/h).
Weights: Empty equipped, 3,675 lb (1 667 kg); max. take-off, 6,600 lb (2 993 kg).
Accommodation: Flight crew of one or two and up to 10 passengers on pairs of bench-type seats.
Status: Prototype flown June 12, 1965, followed by first production aircraft on August 20, 1966. Total of 672 (including Defenders) delivered by beginning of 1977. Production transferred to Fairey SA in Belgium during 1973, the first Belgian-built example being delivered in December of that year, and 315 airframes completed under contract by IRMA in Rumania by early 1977. Eighty Islanders being assembled (20) and part-manufactured (60) in the Philippines.
Notes: The BN-2A-8S features a 45·5-in (1,15-m) longer nose to provide increased baggage space, an additional cabin window each side at the rear, and provision for an additional seat row. These changes, indicated by the suffix "S" (for Stretched), are offered as customer options. A military multi-role version of the Islander (photo) is known as the Defender.

44

BRITTEN-NORMAN BN-2A-8S ISLANDER

Dimensions: Span, 49 ft 0 in (14,94 m); length; 39 ft $5\frac{1}{4}$ in (12,02 m); height, 13 ft 8 in (4,16 m); wing area, 325 sq ft (30,2 m²).

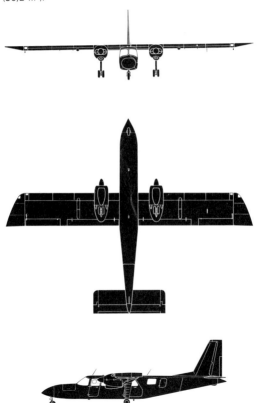

BRITTEN-NORMAN BN-2A MK. III-2 TRISLANDER

Country of Origin: United Kingdom.
Type: Light utility transport and feederliner.
Power Plant: Three 260 hp Avco Lycoming 0-540-E4C5 six-cylinder horizontally-opposed engines.
Performance: Max. speed, 183 mph (294 km²/h) at sea level; cruise at 75% power, 176 mph (283 km/h) at 6,500 ft (1 980 m), at 67% power, 175 mph (282 km/h) at 9,000 ft (2 750 m); range with max. payload, 160 mls (257 km) at 170 mph (274 km/h), with 2,400-lb (1 089-kg) payload, 700 mls (1 127 km) at 175 mph (282 km/h).
Weights: Empty equipped, 5,700 lb (2 585 kg); max. take-off, 10,000 lb (4 536 kg).
Accommodation: Flight crew of one or two, and 16–17 passengers in pairs on bench-type seats.
Status: Prototype flown September 11, 1970, with production prototype flying on March 6, 1971. First production Trislander flown April 29, 1971, and first delivery (to Aurigny) following on June 29, 1971. Trislander production was transferred to Fairey SA at Gosselies, Belgium, late in 1972, and deliveries from the new line began early 1974. Forty-nine Trislanders had been delivered by the beginning of 1977 when production was running at three per month.
Notes: The Trislander is a derivative of the Islander (see pages 44–45) with which it has 75% commonality. The wingtip auxiliary fuel tanks optional on the Islander have been standardised for the Trislander, the extended nose version being known as the Mk. III-2. A military version was under development at the beginning of 1977.

BRITTEN-NORMAN BN-2A TRISLANDER

Dimensions: Span, 53 ft 0 in (16,15 m); length, 43 ft 9 in (13,33 m); height, 14 ft 2 in (4,32 m); wing area, 337 sq ft (31,25 m²).

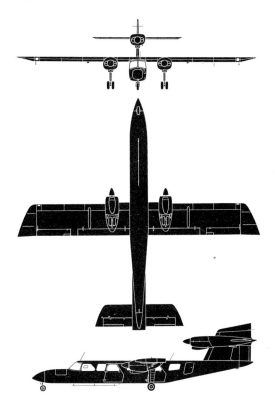

CASA C.101

Country of Origin: Spain.

Type: Two-seat multi-purpose trainer and light tactical aircraft.

Power Plant: One 3,500 lb (1 588 kg) thrust Garrett TFE 731-2-25 turbofan.

Performance: (Estimated) Max. speed, 460 mph (740 km/h) at 20,000 ft (6 095 m), 420 mph (676 km/h) at sea level; initial climb, 4,560 ft/min (23,2 m/sec); service ceiling, 45,000 ft (13 715 m); ferry range, 1,865 mls (3 000 km) at 30 000 ft (9 150 m); endurance, 4 hr 10 min.

Weights: Max. take-off, 10,362 lb (4 700 kg).

Armament: (Armament training and light strike) Up to 4,409 lb (2 000 kg) on seven external stations. One 30-mm cannon or 7,62-mm minigun on fuselage centreline station, alternative loads on six wing stations including six 570-lb (258-kg) MK 82 or four 985-lb (447-kg) MK 83 bombs, six LAU-10 5-in (12,7-cm) or LAU-68 5·75-in (14,6-cm) rockets, six Rockeye II cluster bombs, or four AGM-65 Maverick missiles.

Status: First of four prototypes scheduled to commence test programme in July 1977, with initial deliveries against Spanish Air Force requirement for 60 aircraft commencing late 1979.

Notes: The C.101 is being developed with the co-operation of the Northrop Corporation and Messerschmitt-Bölkow-Blohm, and utilises modular construction in order to facilitate component interchangeability and reduce ground time. Current planning calls for the first complete operational squadron to achieve service status with the Spanish Air Force during 1980, with availability for export from 1981–82.

CASA C.101

Dimensions: Span, 34 ft 9 in (10,6 m); length, 40 ft 2½ in (12,25 m); height, 14 ft 0 in (4,27 m); wing area, 215 sq ft (19,97 m²).

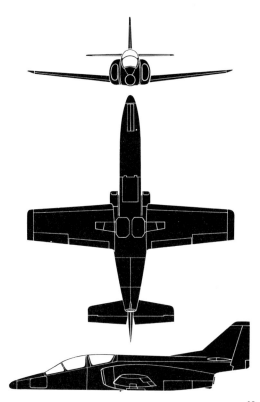

CASA C.212 AVIOCAR

Country of Origin: Spain.

Type: STOL utility transport, navigational trainer and photographic survey aircraft.

Power Plant: Two 776 eshp (715 shp) Garrett-AiResearch TPE 331-5-251C turboprops.

Performance: (At 13,889 lb/6 300 kg) Max. cruise, 243 mph (391 km/h) at 12,000 ft (3 658 m), 238 mph (383 km/h) at 5,000 ft (1 524 m); initial climb, 1,724 ft/min (8,76 m/sec); service ceiling, 24,605 ft (7 500 m); range with max. payload and reserves (30 min hold at 5,000 ft/ 1 524 m plus 5% take-off weight), 205 mls (330 km) at 12,500 ft (3 810 m), with max. fuel, 1,197 mls (1 927 km).

Weights: Empty equipped, 8,045 lb (3 650 kg); max. take-off, 13,889 lb (6 300 kg); max. payload, 4,409 lb (2 000 kg).

Accommodation: Flight crew of two and 18 passengers in commercial configuration. Ten casualty stretchers and three sitting casualties as ambulance. Provision for up to 15 paratroops and jumpmaster or 4,409 lb (2 000 kg) of cargo.

Status: Two prototypes flown March 26 and October 23, 1971, with first of 12 pre-production examples following November 17, 1972. Initial production batch of 32 for Spanish Air Force with deliveries commencing early 1974.

Notes: Of pre-production series, eight have been delivered to Air Force (six for photo survey as C.212Bs and two as C.212E navigational trainers), and the initial production batch has been delivered as C.212A utility transports. Orders have included 22 C.212As and two C.212Bs for Portugal, four C.212As for Jordan and 16 C.212As and commercial C.212Cs for Indonesia, where part-manufacture and assembly are being undertaken.

CASA C.212 AVIOCAR

Dimensions: Span, 62 ft 4 in (19,00 m); length, 49 ft $10\frac{1}{2}$ in (15,20 m); height, 20 ft $8\frac{3}{4}$ in (6,32 m); wing area, 430·556 sq ft (40,0 m²).

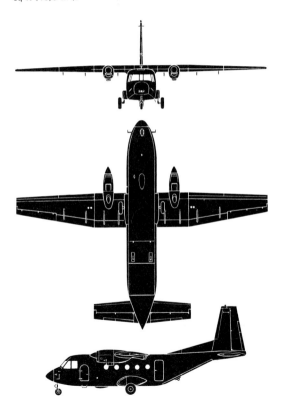

CESSNA 441 CONQUEST

Country of Origin: USA.

Type: Light business executive aircraft.

Power Plant: Two 620 shp Garrett-AiResearch TPE-331-8-401S turboprops.

Performance: Max. speed, 330 mph (532 km/h) at 16,000 ft (4 877 m); max. cruise, 328 mph (528 km/h) at 17,000 ft (5 182 m); range at max. cruise with 45 min reserves (10 occupants), 1,543 mls (2 483 km) at 33,000 ft (10 058 m), 869 mls (1 398 km) at 17,000 ft (5 182 m), (five occupants), 2,106 mls (3 389 km) at 33,000 ft (10 058 m), 1,335 mls (2 148 km) at 17,000 ft (5 182 m); initial climb, 2,405 ft/min (12,2 m/sec); service ceiling, 33,200 ft (10 120 m).

Weights: Empty, 5,487 lb (2 489 kg); max. take-off, 9,850 lb (4 468 kg).

Accommodation: Two seats side by side in cockpit and maximum of eight individual seats in pairs in main cabin.

Status: Prototype flown on August 26, 1975, with initial customer deliveries scheduled June 1977 as part of the Cessna 1978 Model range. Tooling is in preparation for the production of 15 Conquests per month.

Notes: Intended to fit into the market between existing piston-engined twins and turbofan-powered business aircraft, the Conquest is Cessna's first turboprop-powered type to attain production status.

52

CESSNA 441 CONQUEST

Dimensions: Span, 49 ft $3\frac{3}{5}$ in (15,00 m); length, 39 ft $0\frac{1}{4}$ in (11,89 m); height, 13 ft 1 in (3,99 m); wing area, 253 sq ft (23,5 m²).

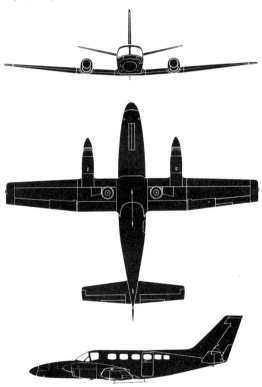

CESSNA CITATION II

Country of Origin: USA.
Type: Light business executive transport.
Power Plant: Two 2,500 lb (1 135 kg) Pratt & Whitney (Canada) JT15D-4 turbofans.
Performance: (Estimated) Max. cruise, 420 mph (676 km/h) at 25,400 ft (7 740 m); range (with 10 persons and 45 min reserves), 2,080 mls (3 347 km); initial climb, 3,500 ft/min (17,8 m/sec); max. altitude, 43,000 ft (13 115 m).
Weights: Typical empty, 6,960 lb (3 160 kg); max. take-off, 12,500 lb (5 675 kg).
Accommodation: Crew of two on separate flight deck and accommodation for up to 10 passengers in main cabin.
Status: The Citation II is scheduled to join the Citation I in production during the last half of 1977 for customer deliveries commencing February 1978, the Citation I having been introduced in December 1976 with the 350th Citation airframe.
Notes: The Citation II is a stretched development of the basic Citation design (which first flew in prototype form on September 15, 1969) and is intended to complement the Citation I which is itself a refined version of the Citation 500 (see 1976 edition) with improved turbofans and a longer span wing (47 ft 1 in/14,36 m as compared with 43 ft 11 in/13,39 m). The Citation II features a lengthened fuselage and still greater wing span, uprated engines and increased fuel capacity. A third member of the Citation range of business executive transports announced in 1976 is the Citation III which, virtually a totally new design, will be a 10–15 seat long-range aircraft and will appear in 1980.

54

CESSNA CITATION II

Dimensions: Span, 51 ft 8 in (15,76 m); length, 47 ft 3 in (14,41 m); height, 14 ft 11 in (4,55 m).

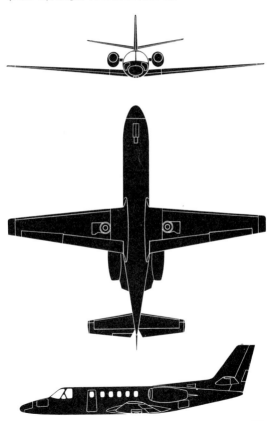

CRANFIELD A1 CHASE

Country of Origin: United Kingdom.
Type: Single-seat aerobatic competition aircraft.
Power Plant: One 210 hp Rolls-Royce/Continental IO-360D six-cylinder horizontally-opposed engine.
Performance: (At 2,020 lb/920 kg) Max. speed, 152 mph (244 km/h); initial climb rate, 1,440 ft/min (7,3 m/sec).
Weights: Max. aerobatic, 1,690 lb (770 kg); max. take-off, 2,020 lb (920 kg).
Status: First example flown on August 23, 1976.
Notes: The A1, built by the College of Aeronautics at Cranfield, is the first aircraft built in the UK solely for aerobatic flying at world championship level, and makes interesting comparison with the Mudry CAP 20L (see pages 156–57), the Yak-50 (pages 214–215) and the Zlin Z.50L (pages 216–217). Designed to an ultimate stress of 13·5 g, which, at a factor of 1·5, is equivalent to +9 g and −6 g, the A1 is of relatively simple and extremely robust construction, and to save weight there are no flaps and no systems—even starting relies on an external source of power. It possesses a designed airframe life of not less than 2,000 hours, half of which may be accumulated in fully aerobatic flight without exceeding the fatigue limits. For competition flying, the aircraft is required to have only a single seat, but provision has been made for a second seat in an optional front cockpit for training and ferry flights. Wheel spats are to be fitted at a later stage in the flight development programme of the aircraft. The A1 Chase programme is managed by Flight Invert Limited, a non-profit-making company.

CRANFIELD A1 CHASE

Dimensions: Span, 32 ft 9½ in (10,00 m); length, 26 ft 5 in (8,05 m); height, 8 ft 10½ in (2,70 m); wing area, 161 sq ft (15,00 m²).

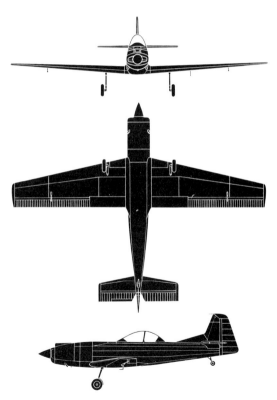

DASSAULT-BREGUET FALCON 10

Country of Origin: France.

Type: Light business executive transport.

Power Plant: Two 3,230 lb (1 465 kg) Garrett-AiResearch TFE-731-2 turbofans.

Performance: Max. cruise, 567 mph (912 km/h) at 30,000 ft (9 145 m), 495 mph (796 km/h) or Mach 0·75 at 45,000 ft (13 716 m); range with four passengers and 45 min reserves, 2,070 mls (3 330 km) at 45,000 ft (13 716 m), 1,495 mls (2 405 km) at max. cruise at 30,000 ft (9 145 m).

Weights: Empty equipped, 10,760 lb (4 880 kg); max. take-off, 18,740 lb (8 500 kg).

Accommodation: Flight crew of two with provision for third crew member on jump seat. Executive version for four passengers with alternative arrangement for seven passengers.

Status: First of three prototypes flown December 1, 1970, followed by second on October 15, 1971, and third on October 16, 1972. The first production Falcon 10 was flown on April 30, 1973, and production deliveries began during November of that year, output being two per month at the beginning of 1977 when some 110 aircraft had been ordered.

Notes: The Falcon 10 (also known as the Mystère 10) is basically a scaled-down version of the Falcon 20 (see 1974 edition), and at a later stage in development it is proposed to offer the 2,980 lb (1 350 kg) Turboméca-SNECMA Larzac turbofan as an alternative power plant. The Falcon 10 is being offered to the *Armée de l'Air* as a military crew trainer and liaison aircraft, and two examples have been delivered to France's *Aéronavale* (which has an option on three more) primarily for radar training under the designation Falcon 10 MER.

DASSAULT-BREGUET FALCON 10

Dimensions: 42 ft 11 in (13,08 m); length, 45 ft 5$\frac{3}{4}$ in (13,86 m); height, 15 ft 1 in (4,61 m); wing area, 259·4 sq ft 24,1 m²).

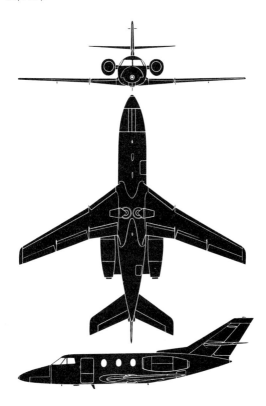

DASSAULT-BREGUET MYSTÈRE 50

Country of Origin: France.

Type: Light business executive transport.

Power Plant: Three 3,700 lb (1 680 kg) Garrett AiResearch TFE 731-3 turbofans.

Performance: Max. cruise, 559 mph (900 km/h) at 29,000 ft (8 840 m) or Mach 0·82; econ. cruise, 491 mph (790 km/h) at 37,000–41,000 ft (11 275–12 495 m) or Mach 0·73; range (45 min reserves and six passengers), 3,604 mls (5 800 km).

Weights: Empty operational, 20,245 lb (9 183 kg); max. take-off, 37,480 lb (17 000 kg).

Accommodation: Flight crew of two and various cabin arrangements for six to ten passengers.

Status: First of three pre-series aircraft flown on November 7, 1976, with second and third scheduled to join the test programme in November 1977 and mid-1978 respectively, with customer deliveries commencing shortly after certification scheduled for September 1978.

Notes: The Mystère 50 (alias Falcon 50) was originally intended to employ the basic fuselage, wing and horizontal tail of the Mystère 20 (Falcon 20) Series F (see 1974 edition), but the decision to undertake major redesign resulted in a one-year delay in the development programme. Further development of the Mystère 50 is expected to include the introduction of TFE 731-4 turbofans of 3,955 lb (1 795 kg) thrust, this uprated power plant being adopted for deliveries of the Mystère 50 subsequent to 1979. The decision to manufacture an initial batch of five production aircraft was taken in June 1976 and a decision concerning follow-on production was scheduled for February 1977.

DASSAULT-BREGUET MYSTÈRE 50

Dimensions: Span, 61 ft 10 in (18,86 m); length, 60 ft 5½ in (18,43 m); height, 18 ft 8 in (5,70 m); wing area; 495 sq ft (46,0 m²).

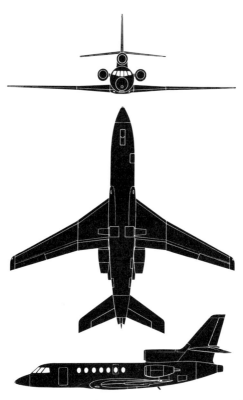

DASSAULT-BREGUET MIRAGE F1

Country of Origin: France.

Type: Single-seat multi-purpose fighter.

Power Plant: One 11,023 lb (5 000 kg) dry and 15,873 lb
(7 200 kg) reheat SNECMA Atar 9K-50 turbojet.

Performance: Max. speed (clean), 915 mph (1 472 km/h)
or Mach 1·2 at sea level, 1,450 mph (2 335 km/h) or Mach
2·2 at 39,370 ft (12 000 m); range cruise, 550 mph (885
km/h) at 29,530 ft (9 000 m); range with max. external
fuel, 2,050 mls (3 300 km), with max. external combat load
of 8,818 lb (4 000 kg), 560 mls (900 km), with external
combat load of 4,410 lb (2 000 kg), 1,430 mls (2 300 km);
service ceiling, 65,600 ft (20 000 m).

Weights: Empty, 16,314 lb (7 400 kg); loaded (clean),
24,030 lb (10 900 kg); max. take-off, 32,850 lb (14 900 kg).

Armament: Two 30-mm DEFA cannon and (intercept) 1-3
Matra 530 Magic and two AIM-9 Sidewinder AAMs.

Status: First of four prototypes flown December 23, 1966.
First of 105 ordered for *Armée de l'Air* flown February 15,
1973. Production rate of four–five per month at beginning
of 1977. Licence manufacture is to be undertaken in South
Africa with deliveries commencing 1977.

Notes: Initial model for *Armée de l'Air* intended primarily for
high-altitude intercept role. Production versions include F1A
and F1E for the ground attack role, the F1B and F1D two-seat
trainers and the F1C interceptor. Fifteen Mirage F1Cs have
been ordered by Spain, 40 by Greece, 25 by Morocco and 20
by Kuwait; delivery of 16 Mirage F1CZ interceptors to South
Africa was completed in 1976, these being followed by 32
Mirage F1AZ ground attack fighters, and 38 (32 Mirage F1As
and F1Es and six two-seat F1Bs and F1Ds) have been ordered
by Libya.

DASSAULT-BREGUET MIRAGE F1

Dimensions: Span, 27 ft 6¾ in (8,40 m); length, 49 ft 2½ in (15,00 m); height, 14 ft 9 in (4,50 m); wing area, 269·098 sq ft (25 m²).

DASSAULT-BREGUET SUPER ÉTENDARD

Country of Origin: France.
Type: Single-seat shipboard strike fighter.
Power Plant: One 11,025 lb (5 000 kg) SNECMA Atar 8K-50 turbojet.
Performance: Max. speed, 745 mph (1 200 km/h) at 985 ft (300 m) or Mach 0·97, 695 mph (1 118 km/h) at 36,000 ft (11 000 m) or Mach 1·05; radius of action (hi-lo-hi with 2,200-lb/998-kg bomb load), 225 mls (360 km), (lo-lo-lo), 160 mls (260 km), (anti-shipping mission with AM-39 Exocet ASM and 1,700-lb/771-kg bomb load), 255 mls (410 km).
Weights: Empty, 13,780 lb (6 250 kg); max. take-off (catapult), 25,350 lb (11 500 kg); overload, 26,455 lb (12 000 kg).
Armament: Two 30-mm DEFA 552A cannon with 122 rpg and a variety of ordnance on five external stores stations (four wing and one fuselage), including Matra 550 Magic AAMs, AM-39 Exocet ASM, etc.
Status: First of three Super Étendard development aircraft (converted from Étendard airframes) flown on October 28, 1974, the second and third flying on March 28 and March 9, 1975, respectively. First production aircraft built against initial contract for 36 scheduled to fly in September 1977. Anticipated production rate of two per month. Total *Aéronavale* requirement for 80 aircraft.
Notes: The Super Étendard is a more powerful derivative of the Étendard IVM (see 1965 edition) with new avionics, a revised wing and other changes. The Super Étendard is intended to serve aboard the carriers Clémenceau and Foch.

DASSULT-BREGUET SUPER ÉTENDARD

Dimensions: Span, 31 ft 6 in (9,60 m); length, 46 ft $11\frac{1}{2}$ in (14,31 m); height, 12 ft 8 in (3,85 m); wing area, 305·7 sq ft (28,40 m²).

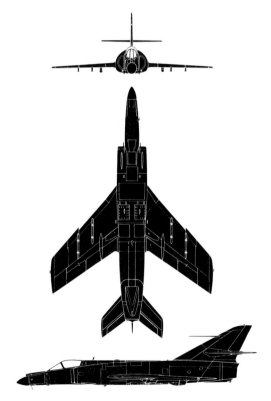

DASSAULT-BREGUET/DORNIER ALPHA JET

Countries of Origin: France and Federal Germany.

Type: Two-seat advanced trainer and light tactical aircraft.

Power Plant: Two 2,975 lb (1 350 kg) SNECMA-Turbo-méca Larzac 04 turbofans.

Performance: Max. speed, 626 mph (991 km/h) at sea level, 560 mph (901 km/h) at 40,000 ft (12 190 m) or Mach 0·85; radius of action (hi-lo-hi), 390 mls (630 km); max. fuel endurance, 2 hrs at sea level, 3 hrs at 32,810 ft (10 000 m); ferry range (max. external fuel), 1,900 mls (3 057 km); initial climb, 11,800 ft/min (59 m/sec); service ceiling, 45,000 ft (13 700 m).

Weights: Empty equipped, 6,944 lb (3 150 kg); operational empty, 7,661 lb (3 475 kg); normal take-off (trainer), 10,780 lb (4 890 kg), (close support), 13,227 lb (6 000 kg); max. overload, 15,432 lb (7 000 kg).

Armament: Provision for external gun pod with 30-mm DEFA 533 cannon or 27-mm Mauser cannon and 150 rounds. Close support version has four wing strong points, inboard points being stressed for loads up to 1,250 lb (570 kg) each and outboard points for loads up to 630 lb (285 kg) each. Maximum external load is 4,850 lb (2 200 kg).

Status: First of four prototypes flown on October 26, 1973 with first series production aircraft scheduled to fly September 1977. First trainer (for *Armée de l'Air*) and first close-support model (for the *Luftwaffe*) to be delivered in July and October 1978 respectively. Approx 200 each for *Armée de l'Air* and *Luftwaffe*, plus 33 (trainers) for Belgium.

Notes: The Alpha Jet is to be built on two final assembly lines (Toulouse and Munich) and is intended for the training role with the *Armée de l'Air* (Alpha Jet E) and close support with the *Luftwaffe* (Alpha Jet A).

DASSAULT-BREGUET/DORNIER ALPHA JET

Dimensions: Span, 29 ft 11 in (9,11 m); length, 40 ft 3 in (12,29 m); height, 13 ft 9 in (4,19 m); wing area, 188 sq ft (17,50 m²).

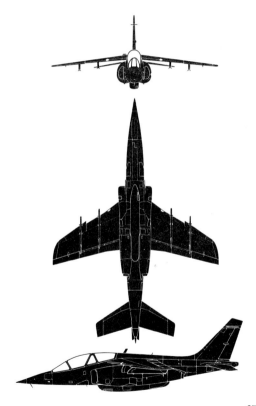

DE HAVILLAND CANADA DHC-5D
BUFFALO

Country of Origin: Canada.

Type: STOL military tactical transport.

Power Plant: Two 3,133 shp General Electric CT64-820-4 turboprops.

Performance: (At 41,000 lb/18 597 kg) Max. cruise, 288 mph (463 km/h) at 10,000 ft (3 050 m); range with 12,000-lb (5 443-kg) payload, 403 mls (649 km), with 18,000-lb (8 165-kg) payload, 690 mls (1 110 km), with zero payload, 2,038 mls (3 280 km); initial climb, 2,330 ft/min (11,8 m/sec).

Weights: Empty operational, 25,000 lb (11 340 kg); max. take-off (assault mission), 41,000 lb (18 597 kg), (transport STOL), 49,200 lb (22 317 kg).

Accommodation: Flight crew of three and 41 fully-equipped troops or 24 casualty stretchers plus six medical attendants/seated casualties.

Status: First DHC-5D flown August 1, 1975, this being one of initial batch of 19 aircraft built against orders which included three for Zaïre, two for Togo, two for Ecuador, four for Kenya and seven for Zambia, all of which were fulfilled during 1976. A further batch of 24 DHC-5Ds was being laid down at the beginning of 1977.

Notes: The DHC-5D embodies uprated engines, minor structural changes and increases in maximum payload and gross weight by comparison with the DHC-5A (see 1972 edition), production of which was phased out in 1972 after the completion of 59 aircraft, production being resumed with the DHC-5D in 1974. The DHC-5D can perform routine STOL operations with 12,000 lb (5 443 kg) of cargo from 1,000-ft (305-m) unimproved strips.

DE HAVILLAND CANADA DHC-5D BUFFALO

Dimensions: Span, 96 ft 0 in (29,26 m); length, 79 ft 0 in (24,08 m); height, 28 ft 8 in (8,73 m); wing area, 945 sq ft (87,8 m²).

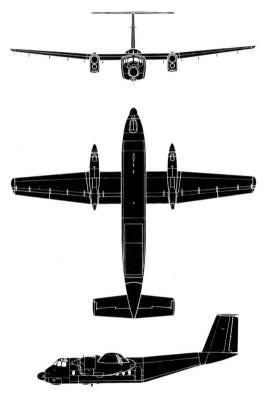

DE HAVILLAND CANADA DHC-7
DASH-7

Country of Origin: Canada.
Type: STOL short-haul commercial transport.
Power Plant: Four 1,120 shp Pratt & Whitney (Canada)
PT6A-50 turboprops.
Performance: Max. cruise, 281 mph (452 km/h) at 15,000
ft (4 570 m); long-range cruise, 259 mph (416 km/h) at 20,000
ft (6 560 m); range (at 80% max. cruise with max. passenger
payload and reserves), 935 mls (1 504 km); max. range (with
7,080-lb/3 211-kg payload at 80% max. cruise), 1,425 mls
(2 293 km).
Weights: Operational empty, 25,860 lb (11 730 kg); max.
take-off, 43,000 lb (19 504 kg).
Accommodation: Flight crew of two and standard seating
for 50 passengers in pairs on each side of central aisle.
Status: Two pre-production aircraft flown on March 27 and
June 26, 1975. The first production aircraft was scheduled for
completion early 1977, with the second following one month
later. Production tempo will attain two per month by 1978.
Twenty-five ordered by beginning of 1977.
Notes: The Dash-7 is jointly funded by de Havilland Canada,
United Technologies (manufacturer of the engines) and the
Canadian government, and was scheduled to achieve certifica-
tion in April 1977, customer deliveries commencing shortly
thereafter. A proposed maritime surveillance version, the Dash-
7R Ranger, was under development at the beginning of 1977.

DE HAVILLAND CANADA DHC-7 DASH-7

Dimensions: Span, 93 ft 0 in (28,35 m); length, 80 ft 7¾ in (24,58 m); height, 26 ft 2 in (7,98 m); wing area, 860 sq ft (79,9 m²).

EMBRAER EMB-111

Country of Origin: Brazil.

Type: Maritime patrol and coastal surveillance aircraft.

Power Plant: Two 750 shp Pratt & Whitney (Canada) PT6A-34 turboprops.

Performance: (Estimated) Max. speed, 280 mph (450 km/h) at 15,000 ft (4 575 m); econ cruise, 225 mph (362 km/h) at 15,000 ft (4 575 m); initial climb, 1,900 ft/min (9,65 m/sec); range, 1,750–1,850 mls (2 816–2 977 km); endurance, 7·5–8·5 hrs.

Weights: Basic operational, 9,259 lb (4 200 kg); max. take-off, 13,558 lb (6 150 kg).

Accommodation: Basic crew of six comprising pilot, co-pilot, navigator, radar operator and two observers.

Status: Sixteen EMB-111s ordered in 1976 for the Brazilian Air Force, including two prototypes, the first of which was scheduled to fly early 1977. Production deliveries expected to commence during the course of 1978.

Notes: The EMB-111 is a derivative of the EMB-110 Bandeirante light utility transport (see 1975 edition) developed to meet the requirements of a specification framed by the Brazilian Air Force's Coastal Command. Range is extended by the use of fixed wingtip tanks, AN/APS-128 patrol search radar is mounted in the nose, a 10-million candlepower searchlight is mounted in a ventral pod, a flare chute is provided in the rear cabin for launching smoke grenades and provision is made for air-to-surface rockets beneath the wings.

EMBRAER EMB-111

Dimensions: Span, 51 ft 5¾ in (15,69 m); length, 48 ft 3¼ in (14,71 m); height, 15 ft 6¼ in (4,73 m); wing area, 312 sq ft (29,00 m²).

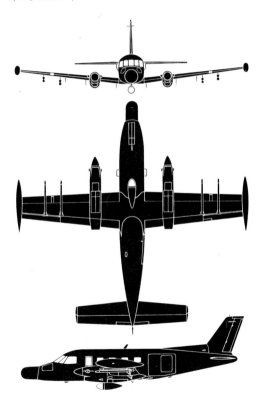

EMBRAER EMB-121 XINGU

Country of Origin: Brazil.

Type: Light business executive transport.

Power Plant: Two 680 shp Pratt & Whitney (Canada) PT6A-28 turboprops.

Performance: (Estimated) Max. speed (at 11,464 lb/5 200 kg), 290 mph (467 km/h) at 15,000 ft (4 570 m); econ. cruise, 242 mph (389 km/h) at 15,000 ft (4 570 m); range (with max. payload), 1,497 mls (2 410 km), (with max. fuel), 1,612 mls (2 595 km); max. initial climb, 1,900 ft/min (9,65 m/sec).

Weights: Empty equipped, 7,000 lb (3 175 kg); max. take-off, 12,346 lb (5 600 kg).

Accommodation: Two seats side-by-side on flight deck and six–seven passengers in individual seats in main cabin.

Status: The first prototype Xingu commenced its flight test programme in November 1976, customer deliveries being scheduled to commence in the second half of 1977.

Notes: The Xingu is the first of the EMB-12X series of pressurised light transports evolved from the EMB-110 Bandeirante (see 1975 edition), further developments being the 10-passenger EMB-123 Tapajós and the 20-passenger EMB-120 Araguaia. By comparison with the Bandeirante, the Xingu has a shorter, pressurised fuselage, but both the Tapajós and the Araguaia will feature a supercritical wing and will be powered by 1,120 shp PT6A-45 turboprops. Both will have an essentially similar fuselage to that of the Xingu, the fuselage length of the Tapajós being stretched to 46 ft 11 in (13,30 m) and that of the Araguaia to 52 ft 11 in (16,13 m). Both the Tapajós and the Araguaia are expected to enter flight testing during the course of 1978.

EMBRAER EMB-121 XINGU

Dimensions: Span, 46 ft 4¾ in (14,14 m); length, 40 ft 5 in (12,32 m); height, 16 ft 2½ in (4,94 m); wing area, 296 sq ft (27,50 m²).

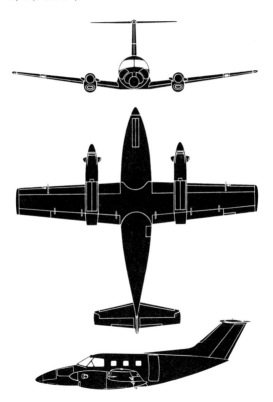

FAIRCHILD A-10A

Country of Origin: USA.

Type: Single-seat close-support aircraft.

Power Plant: Two 9,065 lb (4 112 kg) General Electric TF34-GE-100 turbofans.

Performance: Max. speed (clean), 424 mph (682 km/h) at sea level; max. continuous cruise, 397 mph (639 km/h) at 5,000 ft (1 525 m); loiter endurance (288 mls/463 km from base with 18 500-lb/227-kg Mk 82 bombs and 750 rounds of 30-mm ammunition), 1·8 hrs; terry range (max. fuel and no headwind), 3,015 mls (4 852 km).

Weights: Operational empty, 24,200 lb (10 977 kg); max. take-off, 47,400 lb (21 500 kg).

Armament: One seven-barrel 30-mm General Electric GAU-8 Avenger rotary cannon with up to 1,350 rounds. Max. external ordnance load on 11 pylons (eight under wings and three under fuselage) with full internal fuel and 750 rounds of 30-mm ammunition, 9,540 lb (4 327 kg).

Status: First of two prototypes flown May 10, 1972 and first of six pre-production aircraft flown February 15, 1975. Initial production contracts for 195 placed by beginning of 1977 against planned procurement of 733 (including four refurbished pre-production aircraft) for USAF. First production A-10A flown October 21, 1975, with some 17 delivered by beginning of 1977 when production rate was two per month. Peak production rate of 15 per month scheduled for 1979.

Notes: First USAF Tactical Air Command operational unit to be equipped with the A-10A, the 354th Tactical Fighter Wing, is to be formed in January 1979, and five operational wings are to be formed, each with four 18-aircraft squadrons.

FAIRCHILD A-10A

Dimensions: Span, 57 ft 6 in (17,53 m); length, 54 ft 4 in (16,56 m); height, 14 ft 8 in (4,47 m); wing area, 506 sq ft (47,01 m²).

FOKKER F27 MARITIME

Country of Origin: Netherlands.

Type: Medium-range maritime patrol and surveillance aircraft.

Power Plant: Two 2,250 eshp Rolls-Royce Dart 536-7R turboprops.

Performance: Cruising speed (at 40,000 lb/18 145 kg), 265 mph (427 km/h) at 20,000 ft (6 095 m); typical search speed, 168 mph (270 km/h) at 2,000 ft (610 m); service ceiling (at 45,000 lb/20 412 kg), 23,000 ft (7 010 m); max. range (cruising at 20,000 ft/6 095 m with 30 min loiter and 5% reserves, with pylon tanks), 2,548 mls (4 100 km); max. endurance, 11 hrs.

Weights: Typical zero fuel, 28,097 lb (12 745 kg); max. take-off, 44,996 lb (20 410 kg).

Accommodation: Standard accommodation for crew of six comprising pilot, co-pilot, navigator, radar operator and two observers.

Status: Prototype F27 Maritime (converted F27 Mk 100 No. 68) flown on March 25, 1976, and first production aircraft scheduled for summer 1977 delivery. Initial customer is the Peruvian Navy (2).

Notes: Derivative of Mk 400 transport with Litton AN/APS-503F search radar, Litton LTN-72 long-range inertial navigation system, blister windows adjacent to marine marker launcher and provision for pylon fuel tanks.

FOKKER F27 MARITIME

Dimensions: Span, 95 ft 1$\frac{4}{5}$ in (29,00 m); length, 77 ft 3$\frac{1}{2}$ in (23,56 m); height, 28 ft 6$\frac{7}{10}$ in; wing area, 753·47 sq ft (70.00 m²).

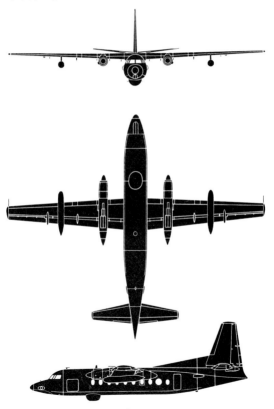

FOKKER F.28 FELLOWSHIP MK. 6000

Country of Origin: Netherlands.

Type: Short-haul commercial transport.

Power Plant: Two 9,850 lb (4 468 kg) Rolls-Royce RB.183-2 Spey Mk. 555-15H turbofans.

Performance: Max. cruise, 523 mph (843 km/h) at 23,000 ft (7 000 m); econ. cruise, 421 mph (678 km/h) at 30,000 ft (9 150 m); range (high-speed schedule), 1,036 mls (1 667 km), (long-range schedule), 1,185 mls (1 908 km); max. cruise altitude, 35,000 ft (10 675 m).

Weights: Operational empty, 38,345 lb (17 393 kg); max. take-off, 70,800 lb (32 115 kg).

Accommodation: Flight crew of two or three. Main cabin layout may be varied to accommodate 55, 60, 65 or 79 passengers in five-abreast seating.

Status: The prototype Fellowship Mk. 6000 (the fuselage of the prototype Mk. 2000 and the modified wings of the second Mk. 1000 prototype) flew September 27, 1973. First production aircraft obtained Certificate of Airworthiness on November 5, 1975, when production of all versions of the Fellowship was running at two per month. A total of some 120 Fellowships had been ordered by the beginning of 1977.

Notes: The Fellowship Mk. 6000 is a derivative of the stretched-fuselage Mk. 2000, offering improved field performance and payload/range capabilities. Wing span is increased by 4 ft 11½ in (1,50 m), three-section leading-edge slats have been added to each wing and an improved version of the Spey engine has been adopted. Planned similar changes to the basic (shorter-fuselage) Fellowship Mk. 1000 were to result in the Mk. 5000, but this development was shelved early in 1976.

FOKKER F.28 FELLOWSHIP MK. 6000

Dimensions: Span, 82 ft 3 in (25,07 m); length, 97 ft 1¾ in (29,61 m); height, 27 ft 9½ in (8,47 m); wing area, 850 sq ft (78,97 m²).

FORGER*

Country of Origin: USSR.

Type: Single-seat VTOL shipboard strike and reconnaissance fighter, and (Forger-B) two-seat conversion trainer.

Power Plant: One (estimated) 18,000–20,000 lb (8 165–9 070 kg) vectored L-thrust turbofan plus two 3,000–3,500 lb (1 360–1 590 kg) lift turbojets.

Performance: (Estimated) Max. speed, 695 mph (1 120 km/h) above 36,000 ft (10 970 m) or Mach 1·05, 725 mph (1 167 km/h) or Mach 0·95 at sea level; cruise, 595 mph (958 km/h) at 20,000 ft (6 095 m) or Mach 0·85; tactical radius (internal fuel), 300 mls (480 km).

Weights: (Estimated) Loaded (clean), 21,500 lb (9 752 kg).

Armament: One 23-mm twin-barrel GSh-23 cannon and bombs or rockets on four underwing pylons.

Status: The Forger is believed to have flown in prototype form in 1971 and attained preliminary service status with the Soviet Naval Air Force during 1976.

Notes: *The design bureau responsible for the development of this aircraft was not known with certainty at the time of closing for press. The Forger was first revealed when the Soviet Navy's new 35,000-ton aircraft carrier, the *Kiev*, passed through the Bosporus and entered the Mediterranean in July 1976. The configuration of the vectoring nozzles behind the wing, balanced by two downward-blowing direct lift engines behind the cockpit, suggests that the Forger is restricted to VTOL operation (i.e., incapable of STOL modes). The aircraft deployed aboard the *Kiev* during 1976 were believed to be a service test quantity and included a tandem two-seat conversion training version (Forger-B) with an overall length of some 58 ft (17,68 m).

FORGER

Dimensions: (Estimated) Span, 23 ft 0 in (7,00 m); length, 50 ft 0 in (15,24 m); wing area, 207 sq ft (19,23 m²).

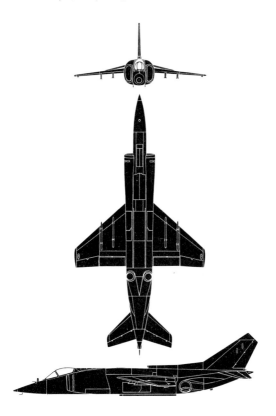

FUJI T-3 (KM-2B)

Country of Origin: Japan.

Type: Tandem two-seat primary trainer.

Power Plant: One 340 hp Avco Lycoming IGSO-480-A1A6 six-cylinder horizontally-opposed engine.

Performance: Max. speed, 234 mph (376 km/h) at 16,000 ft (4 877 m); max. cruise, 204 mph (328 km/h) at 8,000 ft (2 438 m); econ. cruise, 158 (254 km/h) at 8,000 ft (2 438 m); max. range, 645 mls (1 037 km); max. climb rate, 1,520 ft/min (7,62 m/sec); service ceiling, 26,800 ft (8 170 m).

Weights: Empty, 2,470 lb (1 120 kg); max. take-off, 3,330 lb (1 510 kg).

Status: Prototype flown on September 26, 1974, with production of an initial batch of aircraft scheduled to commence during 1977 against planned Air Self-Defence Force procurement of 60 aircraft.

Notes: The T-3 (KM-2B) is the result of two decades of Japanese development of the Beechcraft B45 Mentor, licence manufacture of 126 examples of which was undertaken by Fuji after assembly of 50 from components supplied by the parent manufacturer. A Fuji-developed side-by-side two-seat derivative of the Mentor, the LM-1, was flown in July 1955, 27 being built for the Ground Self-Defence Force, a more powerful development, the KM Super Nikko, following in December 1958. The Super Nikko was subsequently adopted by the Maritime Self-Defence Force as the KM-2 side-by-side basic trainer and the T-3 alias KM-2B is an updated, tandem-seat development.

FUJI T-3 (KM-2B)

Dimensions: Span, 32 ft $9\frac{7}{8}$ in (10,00 m); length, 26 ft $4\frac{1}{2}$ in (8,04 m); height, 9 ft $10\frac{7}{8}$ in (3,02 m); wing area, 177·6 sq ft (16,50 m²).

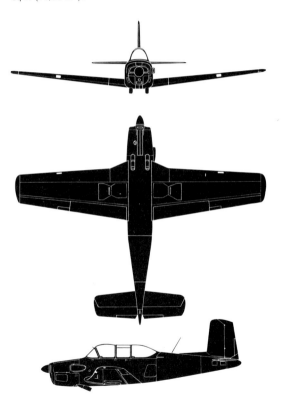

GAF NOMAD N24

Country of Origin: Australia.
Type: STOL military and commercial utility transport.
Power Plant: Two 400 shp Allison 250-B17B turboprops.
Performance: Max. continuous cruise, 193 mph (311 km/h) at sea level, 196 mph (315 km/h) at 5,000 ft (1 525 m); long-range cruise, 167 mph (269 km/h); max. range (with 45 min reserves), 985 mls (1 585 km) at 10,000 ft (3 050 m); initial climb, 1,410 ft/min (7,16 m/sec).
Weights: Empty, 4,549 lb (2 063 kg); max. take-off, 8,500 lb (3 865 kg).
Accommodation: Flight crew of one or two and individual seats for 16 passengers. Three casualty stretchers and eight seated casualties/medical attendants for aeromedical role.
Status: First Nomad N24 (built on production tooling) flown January 1976 with deliveries from mid-1976. By beginning of 1977 production of 120 Nomads (all versions) had been authorised.
Notes: Nomad N24 is stretched version of N22 (see 1976 edition) with 24 in (61 cm) increase in nose length and 45 in (1,14 m) lengthening of the cabin. The N24A with uprated engines will have a max. take-off weight of 9,000 lb (4 082 kg). Current production models of the Nomad include the N22 Mission Master military utility version with self-sealing fuel tanks and provision for underwing hardpoints, and the civil N22B, a float version of which is under development.

GAF NOMAD N24

Dimensions: Span, 54 ft 0 in (16,46 m); length, 47 ft 1 in (14,35 m); height, 18 ft 1½ in (5,52 m); wing area, 324 sq ft (30,10 m²).

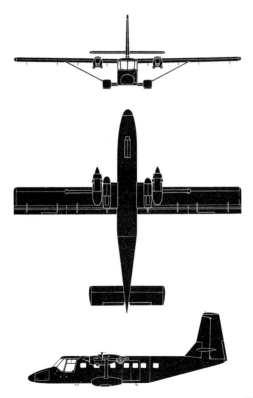

GATES LEARJET 35A

Country of Origin: USA.

Type: Light business executive transport.

Power Plant: Two 3,500 lb (1 588 kg) Garrett AiResearch TFE 731-2 turbofans.

Performance: Max. speed, 565 mph (910 km/h) or Mach 0·83; max. cruise, 534 mph (859 km/h); normal cruise, 507 mph (816 km/h); range (with four passengers and 45 min reserves), 2,858 mls (4 600 km); initial climb, 5,100 ft/min (25,9 m/sec); time to 41,000 ft (12 500 m), 18 min.

Weights: Empty equipped, 8,802 lb (3 992 kg); max. take-off, 17,000 lb (7 711 kg).

Accommodation: Two pilots or pilot and passenger on flight deck and up to seven passengers in main cabin.

Status: Prototype Learjet 35 flown on August 22, 1973, with first customer delivery in November 1974. Succeeded by Learjet 35A from summer of 1976 as one of the so-called Century III series of Learjets. The 600th Learjet was delivered at the beginning of May 1976, and production (all versions) was scheduled to have attained 10 per month by the beginning of 1977.

Notes: The Century III series of Learjets announced October 28, 1975, for mid-1976 delivery feature a modified aerofoil and other aerodynamic improvements. Six models are available: the Learjet 24E and 24F with General Electric CJ610-6 turbojets of 2,950 lb (1 340 kg), the similarly-powered Learjet 25D and 25F embodying a 4 ft 2 in (1,27 m) fuselage stretch, and the Learjet 35A and 36A with turbofans and marginally enlarged overall dimensions (by comparison with the 25D and 25F). By comparison with the 35A, the Learjet 36A has increased fuel capacity resulting in a range of 3,410 miles (5 488 km) with four passengers and reserves.

GATES LEARJET 35A

Dimensions: Span, 39 ft 8 in (12,09 m); length, 48 ft 8 in (14,83 m); height, 12 ft 3 in (3,73 m); wing area, 253·3 sq ft (23,5 m²).

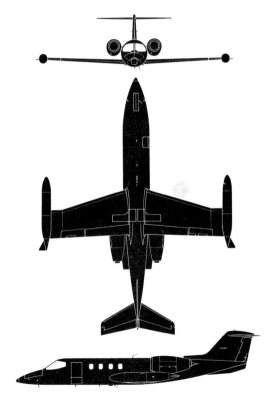

GENERAL DYNAMICS F-16A

Country of Origin: USA.

Type: Single-seat air combat fighter (F-16A) and two-seat operational trainer (F-16B).

Power Plant: One (approx.) 25,000 lb (11 340 kg) reheat Pratt & Whitney F100-PW-100(3) turbofan.

Performance: Max. speed (with two Sidewinder AAMs), 1,255 mph (2 020 km/h) at 36,000 ft (10 970 m) or Mach 1·95, 915 mph (1 472 km/h at sea level or Mach 1·2; tactical radius (interdiction mission hi-lo-hi on internal fuel with six Mk. 82 bombs), 340 mls (550 km); ferry range, 2,300+ mls (3 700+ km); initial climb, 62,000 ft/min (315 m/sec); service ceiling, 52,000 ft (15 850 m).

Weights: Operational empty, 14,100 lb (6 395 kg); loaded (full internal fuel), 22,200 lb (10 070 kg); max. take-off, 33,000 lb (14 969 kg).

Armament: One 20-mm M-61A-1 Vulcan rotary cannon with 500 rounds and up to 11,000 lb (4 990 kg) of stores on nine external (two wingtip, six underwing and one fuselage) stores stations, or 15,200 lb (6 894 kg) with reduced internal fuel.

Status: First of two (YF-16) prototypes flown on January 20, 1974. First of eight pre-production aircraft (six single-seat F-16As and two two-seat F-16Bs) flown December 8, 1976. Planned USAF procurement of 650 aircraft. Total of 348 on order or option for four European NATO countries as follows: Netherlands (84 plus 18 on option), Belgium (102 plus 14 on option), Denmark (48 plus 10 on option) and Norway (72). First production F-16A for USAF scheduled to be completed August 1978.

Notes: YF-16 selected in preference to Northrop YF-17 (see 1975 edition) to meet USAF's Air Combat Fighter requirement.

GENERAL DYNAMICS F-16A

Dimensions: Span (excluding missiles), 31 ft 0 in (9,45 m);
length, 47 ft 7¾ in (14,52 m); height, 16 ft 5¼ in (5,01 m);
wing area, 300 sq ft (27,87 m²).

GRUMMAN A-6E INTRUDER

Country of Origin: USA.

Type: Two-seat shipboard low-level strike aircraft.

Power Plant: Two 9,300 lb (4 218 kg) Pratt & Whitney J52-P-8A/B turbojets.

Performance: Max. speed (clean), 654 mph (1 052 km/h) at sea level or Mach 0·86, 625 mph (1 006 km/h) at 36,000 ft (10 970 m) or Mach 0·94, (close support role with 28 Mk. 81 Snakeye bombs), 557 mph (896 km/h) at 5,000 ft (1 525 m); combat range (clean), 2,320 mls (3 733 km) at 482 mph (776 km/h) average at 37,700–44,600 ft (11 500–13 600 m).

Weights: Empty, 25,980 lb (11 795 kg); max. take-off (field), 60,400 lb (27 420 kg), (catapult), 58,600 lb (26 605 kg).

Armament: Five external (one fuselage and four wing) stations each of 3,600 lb (1 635 kg) capacity for up to 15,000 lb (6 804 kg) of stores.

Status: Current production version of the Intruder, the A-6E, first flew on February 27, 1970, and as of September 1975, 66 new A-6Es had been built and 104 modified from A-6A standard. Programme called for last of 94 new-build A-6Es to be delivered in February 1976, and conversion of earlier Intruders to A-6E standard (total of 228) to extend through 1979.

Notes: All US Navy and US Marine Corps Intruders are being progressively updated to the latest A-6E standard with TRAM (Target Recognition Attack Multi-sensor) systems, FLIR (Forward-Looking Infra-Red) and CAINS (Carrier Airborne Inertial Navigation System), that illustrated opposite being a new production A-6E with fuselage air brakes deleted and TRAM turret under nose. The Intruder is also being modified to carry the active-seeker Harpoon missile.

GRUMMAN A-6E INTRUDER

Dimensions: Span, 53 ft 0 in (16,15 m); length, 54 ft 9 in (16,69 m); height, 16 ft 2 in (4,93 m); wing area, 528·9 sq ft (49,14 m²).

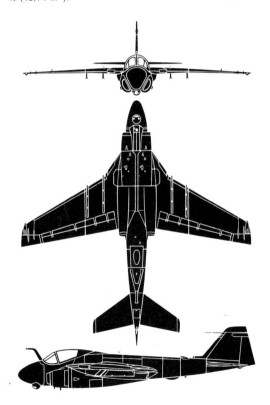

GRUMMAN E-2C HAWKEYE

Country of Origin: USA.

Type: Shipboard airborne early warning, surface surveillance and strike control aircraft.

Power Plant: Two 4,910 ehp Allison T56-A-425 turboprops.

Performance: Max. speed (at max. take-off), 348 mph (560 km/h) at 10,000 ft (3 050 m); max. range cruise, 309 mph (498 km/h); max. endurance, 6·1 hrs; mission endurance (at 230 mls/370 km from base), 4·0 hrs; ferry range, 1,604 mls (2 580 km); initial climb, 2,515 ft/min (12,8 m/sec); service ceiling, 30,800 ft (9 390 m).

Weights: Empty, 38,009 lb (17 240 kg); max. take-off, 51,900 lb (23 540 kg).

Accommodation: Crew of five comprising flight crew of two and Airborne Tactical Data System team of three, each at an independent operating station.

Status: First of two E-2C prototypes flown on January 20, 1971, with first production aircraft flying on September 23, 1972. Thirty-four E-2Cs scheduled for delivery by beginning of Fiscal Year 1977, in which year a further six are to be procured by the US Navy. Four E-2Cs have been ordered by Israel.

Notes: The E-2C is the current production version of the Hawkeye which first flew as an aerodynamic prototype on October 21, 1960. Fifty-nine E-2As were delivered up to 1967 (all subsequently being updated to E-2B standard), development of the E-2C commencing during the following year. All E-2C Hawkeyes delivered subsequent to December 1976 have the new APS-125 advanced radar processing system offering improved overland capability. Israeli Hawkeyes are to have this new equipment.

GRUMMAN E-2C HAWKEYE

Dimensions: Span, 80 ft 7 in (24,56 m); length, 57 ft 7 in (17,55 m); height, 18 ft 4 in (5,59 m); wing area, 700 sq ft (65,03 m²).

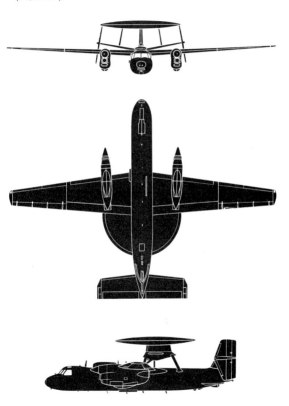

GRUMMAN F-14A TOMCAT

Country of Origin: USA.

Type: Two-seat shipboard multi-purpose fighter.

Power Plant: Two 20,900 lb (9 480 kg) reheat Pratt & Whitney TF30-P-412A turbofans.

Performance: Design max. speed (clean), 1,545 mph (2 486 km/h) at 40,000 ft (12 190 m) or Mach 2·34; max. speed (internal fuel and four AIM-7 missiles at 55,000 lb/24 948 kg), 910 mph (1 470 km/h) at sea level or Mach 1·2; tactical radius (internal fuel and four AIM-7 missiles plus allowance for 2 min combat at 10,000 ft/3 050 m), approx. 450 mls (725 km); time to 60,000 ft (18 290 m) at 55,000 lb (24 948 kg), 2·1 min.

Weights: Empty equipped, 40,070 lb (18 176 kg); normal take-off (internal fuel and four AIM-7 AAMs), 55,000 lb (24 948 kg); max. take-off (ground attack/interdiction), 68,567 lb (31 101 kg).

Armament: One 20-mm M-61A1 rotary cannon and (intercept mission) six AIM-7E/F Sparrow and four AIM-9G/H Sidewinder AAMs or six AIM-54A and two AIM-9G/H AAMs.

Status: First of 12 research and development aircraft flown December 21, 1970, and US Navy plans to acquire a total of 403 by the end of Fiscal Year 1981 of which 270 had been funded up to the end of Fiscal Year 1976. Some 230 had been delivered to the US Navy by the beginning of 1977, together with approximately 30 of total orders for 80 placed on behalf of the Iranian Imperial Air Force.

Notes: The selection of a new engine for the Tomcat is scheduled to be made by the end of 1977, and this will be installed in new production aircraft commencing 1978, with TF30-powered Tomcats being retrofitted from about 1980. A total of 18 US Navy Tomcat-equipped squadrons is currently planned.

GRUMMAN F-14A TOMCAT

Dimensions: Span (max.), 64 ft 1½ in (19,55 m), (min.), 37 ft 7 in (11,45 m), (overswept on deck), 33 ft 3½ in (10,15 m); length, 61 ft 11⅞ in (18,90 m); height, 16 ft 0 in (4,88 m); wing area, 565 sq ft (52,5 m²).

HAL AJEET

Country of Origin: India.

Type: Single-seat lightweight fighter.

Power Plant: One 4,670 lb (2 118 kg) HAL-built Rolls-Royce Bristol Orpheus 701-01 turbojet.

Performance: Max. speed, 665 mph (1 070 km/h) at 20,000 ft (6 095 m) or Mach 0·95; tactical radius (high altitude intercept), 460 mls (740 km), (lo-lo-lo), 150 mls (240 km); max. climb rate, 20,000 ft/min (10,16 m/sec); time to 40,000 ft (12 190 m), 6·0 min.

Weights: Empty, 5,074 lb (2 302 kg); approx. loaded (intercept role), 7,803 lb (3 539 kg); max. take-off, 9,195 lb (4 170 kg).

Armament: Two 30-mm Aden cannon with 90 rpg. Four wing hardpoints for external ordnance, typical external loads including two 500-lb (226,8-kg) bombs or four 18×68-mm Arrow rocket pods.

Status: First Ajeet prototype flown March 6, 1975, with second prototype following in November 1975. First production Ajeet flown May 1976, with first deliveries to the Indian Air Force commencing in last quarter of 1976 against reported requirement for 100 aircraft.

Notes: The Ajeet (Unconquerable) is a refined version of the Hawker Siddeley (Folland) Gnat lightweight fighter, licence manufacture of which was completed by HAL (Hindustan Aeronautics Limited) on January 31, 1974, after completion of 193 aircraft (plus assembly of 20 from components supplied by parent company). By comparison with the Gnat, the Ajeet has integral wing fuel tankage of 110 Imp gal (500 l) capacity, reinforced wings, a zero-level Martin-Baker ejection seat, a Ferranti ISIS weapons aiming system, a new cannon feed system, updated avionics and a marginally more powerful turbojet. The first of two two-seat Ajeet trainers is scheduled to fly in 1978.

HAL AJEET

Dimensions: Span, 22 ft 2 in (6,76 m); length, 29 ft 9 in (9,07 m); height, 8 ft 10 in (2,69 m); wing area, 136·6 sq ft (12,69 m²).

HAL HPT-32

Country of Origin: India.

Type: Side-by-side two-seat primary trainer.

Power Plant: One 260 hp Avco Lycoming AEIO-540-D4B5 six-cylinder horizontally-opposed engine.

Performance: (Estimated at 2,645 lb/1 200 kg) Max. speed, 161 mph (260 km/h) at sea level; range (standard tankage), 620 mls (1 000 km) at 137 mph (220 km/h) at 6,560 ft (2 000 m); max. endurance (with 30 Imp gal/136 l auxiliary tank), 7 hrs.

Weights: Empty, 1,870 lb (850 kg); normal max. take-off, 2,645 lb (1 200 kg).

Armament: For operation as a light counter-insurgency or armament training aircraft four wing hardpoints are provided to carry up to 560 lb (225 kg) of ordnance.

Status: The first of two prototypes commenced its flight test programme on January 6, 1977, with production to be initiated mid-1978 with deliveries to the Indian Air Force commencing during the following year.

Notes: The HPT-32 has been designed as a successor to the HT-2 as a primary trainer in the Indian Air Force. It is anticipated that initial production aircraft will, like the prototypes, be powered by the Avco Lycoming engine but that later aircraft will have a new 260 hp six-cylinder engine currently under development in India. The HPT-32 has provision for an optional third seat or auxiliary fuel tank in the rear of the cabin, and the airframe has been designed for a fatigue life of 6,500 hours.

HAL HPT-32

Dimensions: Span, 31 ft 2 in (9,50 m); length, 25 ft 4 in (7,72 m); height, 9 ft 7½ in (2,93 m); wing area, 161 sq ft (15,00 m²).

HAWKER SIDDELEY 125 SERIES 700

Country of Origin: United Kingdom.
Type: Light business executive transport.
Power Plant: Two 3,700 lb (1 680 kg) Garrett-AiResearch TFE 731-3-1H turbofans.
Performance: High speed cruise, 506 mph (814 km/h); long-range cruise, 460 mph (740 km/h) or Mach 0·7; range (with six passengers and 45 min reserves), 2,660 mls (4 280 km) at Mach 0·7, 2,130 mls (3 427 km) at Mach 0·75.
Weights: Max. take-off, 25,000 lb (11 340 kg).
Accommodation: Normal flight crew of two and basic arrangement for eight passengers.
Status: Series 700 development aircraft (a converted Series 600) first flown on June 28, 1976, with first production aircraft having been flown on November 8, 1976. Deliveries from initial production batch of 20 aircraft to commence in second quarter of 1977 and five had been sold by the beginning of the year.
Notes: The Series 700 differs from the Series 600 (see 1976 edition) that it supplants primarily in having turbofans in place of Viper 601 turbojets, resulting in a 50% increase in range with the same fuel tankage. Various aerodynamic improvements have also been introduced which have resulted in drag reduction of some 3%. The Series 700 was preceded by 72 Series 600 aircraft, 114 Series 400 aircraft and 148 examples of earlier models, plus two prototypes and 20 of a navigational training version (Dominie).

HAWKER SIDDELEY 125 SERIES 700

Dimensions: Span, 47 ft 0 in (14,32 m); length, 50 ft 6 in (15,39 m); height, 17 ft 3 in (5,26 m); wing area, 353 sq ft (32,80 m²).

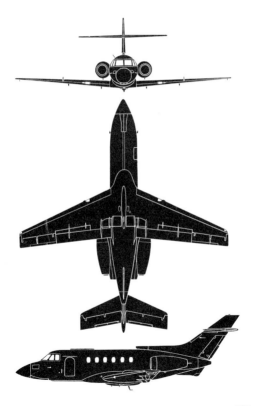

HAWKER SIDDELEY 748 COASTGUARDER

Country of Origin: United Kingdom.

Type: Medium-range maritime patrol and surveillance aircraft.

Power Plant: Two 2,280 ehp Rolls-Royce Dart R.Da.7 Mk 535-2 turboprops.

Performance: (Estimated) Max. cruise (at 40,000 lb/18 145 kg), 278 mph (448 km/h) at 15,000 ft (4 570 m); time on station (at mission radius of 230 mls/370 km), 8·5 hrs; endurance (max. internal fuel) 12 (plus) hrs; max. initial climb, 1,320 ft/min (6,7 m/sec); service ceiling, 25,000 ft (7 620 m).

Weights: Empty, 22,827 lb (10 354 kg); basic operational, 26,393 lb (11 971 kg); normal max. take-off, 46,500 lb (21 092 kg).

Accommodation: Basic crew of five comprising two pilots, a tactical navigator and two observer/despatchers. A routine navigator may be accommodated if required. Stores launch area at rear of cabin with launching chute for flares and sea markers.

Status: Prototype conversion of company-owned HS 748 demonstrator was scheduled to fly February 1977. Production deliveries could commence 1978.

Notes: A derivative of the HS 748 Srs 2A short- to medium-range transport (see 1976 edition), the Coastguarder is, like the Fokker F27 Maritime (see pages 78–79) intended for the protection of offshore energy and fishery resources, anti-smuggling and air-sea rescue roles and for general maritime reconnaissance where a more sophisticated long-range aircraft is not required.

HAWKER SIDDELEY 748 COASTGUARDER

Dimensions: Span, 98 ft 6 in (30,02 m); length, 67 ft 0 in (20,42 m); height, 24 ft 10 in (7,57 m); wing area, 810·75 sq ft (75,35 m²).

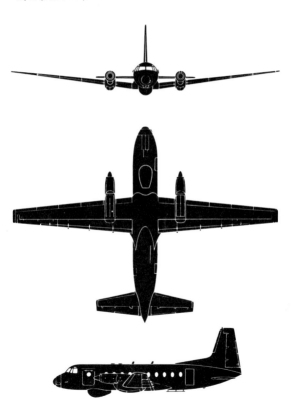

HAWKER SIDDELEY HARRIER G.R. MK. 3

Country of Origin: United Kingdom.
Type: Single-seat V/STOL strike and reconnaissance fighter.
Power Plant: One 21,500 lb (9 760 kg) Rolls-Royce Pegasus 103 vectored-thrust turbofan.
Performance: Max. speed, 720 mph (1 160 km/h) or Mach 0·95 at 1,000 ft (305 m), with typical external ordnance load, 640–660 mph (1 030–1 060 km) or Mach 0·85–0·87 at 1,000 ft (305 m); cruise, 560 mph (900 km/h) or Mach 0·8 at 20,000 ft (6 096 m); tactical radius for hi-lo-hi mission, 260 mls (418 km), with two 100 Imp gal (455 l) external tanks, 400 mls (644 km).
Weights: Empty, 12,400 lb (5 624 kg); max. take-off (VTO), 18,000 lb (8 165 kg); max. take-off (STO), 23,000+ lb (10 433+ kg); approx. max. take-off, 26,000 lb (11 793 kg).
Armament: Provision for two 30-mm Aden cannon with 130 rpg and up to 5,000 lb (2 268 kg) of ordnance.
Status: First of six pre-production aircraft flown August 31, 1966, with first of 77 G.R. Mk. 1s for RAF following December 28, 1967. Production of G.R. Mk. 1s and 13 T. Mk. 2s (see 1969 edition) for RAF completed. Production of 102 Mk. 50s (equivalent to G.R. Mk. 3) and eight Mk. 54 two-seaters (equivalent to T. Mk. 4) for US Marine Corps, and six Mk. 50s and two Mk. 54s ordered (via the USA) by Spain (by which known as Matador). Follow-on order for 15 G.R. Mk. 3s placed March 1973.
Notes: RAF Harrier G.R. Mk. 1s and T. Mk. 2s converted to G.R. Mk. 1As and T. Mk. 2As by installation of 20,000 lb (9 100 kg) Pegasus 102 have been progressively modified as G.R. Mk. 3s and T. Mk. 4s by installation of Pegasus 103 similar to that installed in Mk. 50 (AV-8A) for USMC.

HAWKER SIDDELEY HARRIER G.R. MK. 3

Dimensions: Span, 25 ft 3 in (7,70 m); length, 45 ft 7$\frac{3}{4}$ in (13,91 m); height, 11 ft 3 in (3,43 m); wing area, 201·1 sq ft (18,68 m^2).

HAWKER SIDDELEY SEA HARRIER F.R.S. MK. 1

Country of Origin: United Kingdom.

Type: Single-seat V/STOL shipboard multi-role fighter.

Power Plant: One 21,500 lb (9 760 kg) Rolls-Royce Pegasus 104 vectored-thrust turbofan.

Performance: (Estimated) Max. speed, 720 mph (1 160 km/h) at 1,000 ft (305 m) or Mach 0·95, with typical external stores load, 640–660 mph (1 030–1 060 km/h) or Mach 0·85–0·87; combat air patrol radius (vertical take-off with two 100 Imp gal/455 l drop tanks), 100 mls (160 km) with substantial loiter time.

Weights: Max. take-off (STOL), 25,000 lb (11 339 kg).

Armament: Provision for two (flush-fitting) podded 30-mm Aden cannon with 130 rpg beneath fuselage. Up to 5,000 lb (2 268 kg) of ordnance externally.

Status: First of three development and evaluation Sea Harriers (built on production tooling) scheduled to fly in July 1977, with second and third following in October 1977 and January 1978. Total of 24 ordered with initial service entry scheduled for 1979.

Notes: The Sea Harrier differs from the Harrier of the RAF and USMC (see pages 106–107) primarily in having a redesigned and raised cockpit, a new nose accommodating Ferranti Blue Fox air–air and air–surface radar, and a revised weapons fit. Provision is made for Sidewinder AAMs on the outboard wing pylons, and the Sea Harrier will lift its max. military load from a 500-ft (152,4-m) flight deck with a 30-knot (55 km/hr) over-deck wind.

HAWKER SIDDELEY SEA HARRIER F.R.S. MK. 1

Dimensions: Span, 25 ft 3 in (7,70 m); length, 47 ft 7 in (14,50 m); height, 12 ft 2 in (3,70 m); wing area, 201·1 sq ft (18,68 m²).

HAWKER SIDDELEY HAWK T. MK. 1

Country of Origin: United Kingdom.

Type: Two-seat multi-purpose trainer and light tactical aircraft.

Power Plant: One 5,340 lb (2 422 kg) Rolls-Royce Turboméca RT.172-06-11 Adour 151 turbofan.

Performance: Max. speed, 617 mph (993 km/h) at sea level, 570 mph (917 km/h) at 30,000 ft (9 144 m); range cruise, 405 mph (652 km/h) at 30,000 ft (9 144 m); time to 40,000 ft (12 192 m), 10 min; service ceiling, 44,000 ft (13 410 m).

Weights: Empty, 7,450 lb (3 379 kg); normal take-off (trainer), 10,250 lb (4 649 kg), (weapons trainer), 12,000 lb (5 443 kg); max. take-off, 16,500 lb (7 484 kg).

Armament: (Weapon trainer) One strong point on fuselage centreline and two wing strong points and (ground attack) two additional wing strong points, all stressed for loads up to 1,000 lb (454 kg). Max. external load of 5,000 lb (2 268 kg).

Status: Single pre-production example flown on August 21, 1974, and first and second production examples flown on May 19 and April 22, 1975, respectively. Total of 175 on order for RAF with 10 delivered to that service by 1977 with completion of order in 1980.

Notes: The Hawk is to be used by the RAF in the basic and advanced flying training and weapons training roles, and both single- and two-seat ground attack versions are being offered for export. The projected single-seat version features more internal fuel, an automatic navigation system and various sensors to enhance weapon delivery. In November 1976, the Hawk was selected for service with Finland's air arm, some 50 aircraft being initially involved.

HAWKER SIDDELEY HAWK T. MK. 1

Dimensions: Span, 30 ft 10 in (9,40 m); length (including probe), 39 ft 2½ in (11,96 m); height, 13 ft 5 in (4,10 m); wing area, 180 sq ft (16,70 m²).

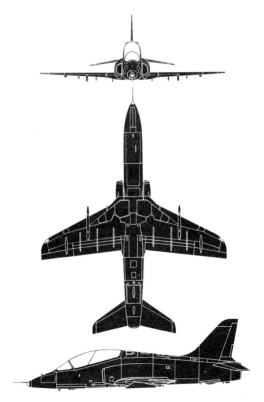

HAWKER SIDDELEY NIMROD M.R. MK. 1

Country of Origin: United Kingdom.

Type: Long-range maritime patrol aircraft.

Power Plant: Four 12,160 lb (5 515 kg) Rolls-Royce RB. 168-20 Spey Mk. 250 turbofans.

Performance: Max. speed, 575 mph (926 km/h); max. transit speed, 547 mph (880 km/h); econ. transit speed, 490 mph (787 km/h); typical ferry range, 5,180–5,755 mls (8 340–9 265 km); typical endurance, 12 hrs.

Weights: Max. take-off, 177,500 lb (80 510 kg); max. overload (eight new-build Mk. 1s), 192,000 lb (87 090 kg).

Armament: Ventral weapons bay accommodating full range of ASW weapons (homing torpedoes, mines, depth charges, etc) plus two underwing pylons on each side for total of four Aérospatiale AS.12 ASMs (or AS.11 training rounds).

Accommodation: Normal operating crew of 12 with two pilots and flight engineer on flight deck and nine navigators and sensor operators in tactical compartment.

Status: First of two Nimrod prototypes employing modified Comet 4C airframes flown May 23, 1967. First of initial batch of 38 production Nimrod M.R. Mk. 1s flown on June 28, 1968. Completion of this batch in August 1972 followed by delivery of three Nimrod R. Mk. 1s for special electronics reconnaissance, and eight more M.R. Mk. 1s on order with deliveries continuing into 1977.

Notes: Entire fleet to undergo refit programme as Nimrod M.R. Mk. 2s with updated avionics and communications fit and service entry from 1978. Changes will include new EMI radar, a new sonics system, a navigation system of improved accuracy, increased computer capacity and improved display system techniques. An aerodynamic test bed for a proposed airborne warning and control system version will commence flight trials during May 1977.

HAWKER SIDDELEY NIMROD M.R. MK. 1

Dimensions: Span, 114 ft 10 in (35,00 m); length, 126 ft 9 in (38,63 m); height, 29 ft 8½ in (9,01 m); wing area, 2,121 sq ft (197,05 m²).

IAI KFIR-C2

Country of Origin: Israel.

Type: Single-seat multi-role fighter.

Power Plant: One 11,870 lb (5 385 kg) dry and 17,900 lb (8 120 kg) Bet-Shemesh-built General Electric J79-GE-17 turbojet.

Performance: (Estimated) Max. speed (50% fuel and two Shafrir AAMs), 850 mph (1 368 km/h) at 1,000 ft (305 m) or Mach 1·12, 1,420 mph (2 285 km/h) above 36,000 ft (10 970 m) or Mach 2·3; max. low-level climb rate, 47,250 ft/min (240 m/sec); max. ceiling, 59,050 ft (18 000 m); radius of action (air superiority mission with two 110 Imp gal/500 l drop tanks), 323 mls (520 km), (ground attack mission hi-lo-hi profile), 745 mls (1 200 km).

(intercept mission with 50% fuel and two AAMs), 20,700 lb (9 390 kg); max. take-off, 32,190 lb (14 600 kg).

Armament: Two 30-mm DEFA cannon with 125 rpg and (intercept) two or four Rafael Shafrir AAMs, or (ground attack) up to 8,820 lb (4 000 kg) of external ordnance.

Status: Initial production version of Kfir delivered to Israeli air arm from April 1975 with deliveries of improved Kfir-C2 scheduled for early 1977. Production rate at beginning of 1977 approx. 2·5 to 3·0 per month.

Notes: The Kfir-C2 differs from initial production Kfir (Young Lion) primarily in having canard auxiliary surfaces, dogtooth wing leading-edge extensions and nose strakes which aid low-speed manoeuvrability. The Kfir is based on the airframe of the Dassault-Breguet Mirage 5.

IAI KFIR-C2

Dimensions: Span, 26 ft $11\frac{1}{2}$ in (8,22 m); length, 51 ft $0\frac{1}{4}$ in (15,55 m); height, 13 ft $11\frac{1}{2}$ in (4,25 m); wing area (excluding canard and dogtooth), 375·12 sq ft (34,85 m²).

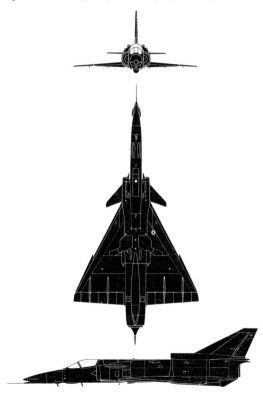

ILYUSHIN IL-38 (MAY)

Country of Origin: USSR.

Type: Long-range maritime patrol aircraft.

Power Plant: Four 4,250 ehp Ivchenko AI-20M turboprops.

Performance: (Estimated) Max. continuous cruise, 400 mph (645 km/h) at 15,000 ft (4 570 m); normal cruise, 370 mph (595 km/h) at 26,250 ft (8 000 m); patrol speed, 250 mph (400 km/h) at 2,000 ft (610 m); max. range, 4,500 mls (7 240 km); loiter endurance, 12 hrs at 2,000 ft (610 m).

Weights: (Estimated) Empty equipped, 80,000 lb (36 287 kg); max. take-off, 140,000 lb (63 500 kg).

Armament: Internal weapons bay for depth bombs, homing torpedoes, etc. Wing hardpoints for external ordnance loads.

Accommodation: Normal flight crew believed to consist of 12 members, of which half are housed by tactical compartment, operating sensors and co-ordinating data flow to surface vessels and other aircraft.

Status: The Il-38 reportedly flew in prototype form during 1967–68, entering service with the Soviet naval air arm early in 1970.

Notes: The Il-38 has been evolved from the Il-18 commercial transport in a similar fashion to the development of the Lockheed P-3 Orion from the Electra transport. Apart from some strengthening, the wings, tail assembly and undercarriage are similar to those of the Il-18. By comparison, the wing is positioned further forward on the fuselage for CG reasons. The Il-38 has been observed operating in the Mediterranean as well as over the seas surrounding the Soviet Union and an initial batch of three aircraft of this type is to be delivered to the Indian Navy during 1977, with a follow-on batch of a further three for 1978–79 delivery.

ILYUSHIN IL-38 (MAY)

Dimensions: Span, 122 ft 9 in (37,40 m); length, 131 ft 0 in (39,92 m); height, 33 ft 4 in (10,17 m); wing area, 1,507 sq ft (140,0 m²).

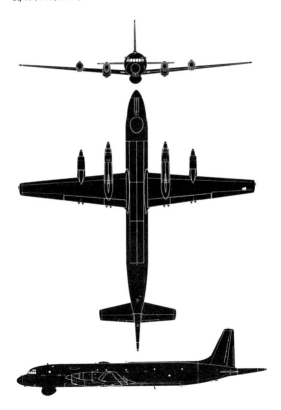

ILYUSHIN IL-76 (CANDID)

Country of Origin: USSR.
Type: Heavy commercial and military freighter.
Power Plant: Four 26,455 lb (12 000 kg) Soloviev D-30KP turbofans.
Performance: Max. cruise, 528 mph (850 km/h) at 42,650 ft (13 000 m); range with max. payload (88,185 lb/40 000 kg), 3,107 mls (5 000 km).
Weights: Max. take-off, 346,122 lb (157 000 kg).
Accommodation: Normal flight crew of three–four with navigator below flight deck in glazed nose. Pressurised hold for containerised and other freight, wheeled and tracked vehicles, etc.
Status: First of four prototypes flown on March 25, 1971, with production deliveries to both Aeroflot and the Soviet Air Forces commencing in 1974.
Notes: The Il-76 is being manufactured in both commercial and military versions, the latter featuring tail warning radar and a tail gun position mounting two 23-mm NR-23 cannon. During the summer of 1975, an Il-76 established 25 new speed-with-load and load-to-altitude records, these including a 154,324-lb (70 000-kg) load over a distance of 621 mls (1 000 km) at an average speed of 532 mph (856 km/h), a similar load to an altitude of 38,959 ft (11 875 m), and a 88,185-lb (40 000-kg) load over a 3,107-mile (5 000-km) closed circuit at an average speed of 507 mph (816 km/h). An aerial refuelling tanker version of the Il-76 is reported to be under development for use with the Backfire bomber.

ILYUSHIN IL-76 (CANDID)

Dimensions: Span, 165 ft 8⅓ in (50,50 m); length, 152 ft 10¼ in (46,59 m); height, 48 ft 5⅛ in (14,76 m); wing area, 3,229·2 sq ft (300,00 m²).

ILYUSHIN IL-86

Country of Origin: USSR.

Type: Medium-haul commercial transport.

Power Plant: Four 28,660 lb (13 000 kg) Soloviev (or Lotarev) turbofans.

Performance: (Estimated) Normal cruise, 572–590 mph (920–950 km/h) at 30,000–33,000 ft (9 000–10 000 m); range with max. payload (88,185 lb/40 000 kg), 1,460 mls (2 350 km), with max. fuel, 2,858 mls (4 600 km).

Weights: Max. take-off, 414,470 lb (188 000 kg).

Accommodation: Flight crew of three–four and up to 350 passengers in basic nine-abreast seating with two aisles (divided between three cabins accommodating 111, 141 and 98 passengers respectively). One proposed mixed-class layout provides for 28 passengers six-abreast in forward cabin and 206 passengers eight-abreast in centre and aft cabins.

Status: Prototype was flown for the first time on December 22, 1976, with Aeroflot service entry expected towards the end of the present decade.

Notes: Evolved under the supervision of General Designer G. V. Novozhilov, the IL-86 is intended for both domestic and international high-density routes. The prototype is believed to be powered by four Soloviev D-30KP turbofans of 26,455 lb (12 000 kg) each, but an uprated turbofan of Soloviev design or a competitive turbofan from the Lotarev bureau is expected to power the initial production version. The IL-86 will be operated by Aeroflot over stage lengths ranging from 500 to 2,360 miles (800 to 3 800 km).

ILYUSHIN IL-86

Dimensions: Span, 158 ft 6 in (48,33 m); length, 191 ft 11 in (58,50 m); height, 51 ft 6 in (15,70 m); wing area, 3,444 sq ft (320,0 m²).

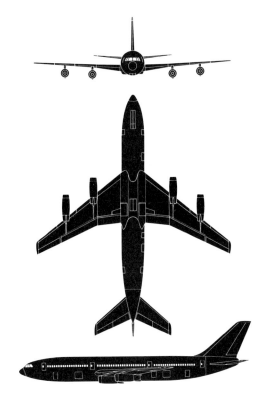

JUROM (IAR 93) ORAO

Countries of Origin: Jugoslavia and Romania.
Type: Single-seat tactical fighter and two-seat operational trainer.
Power Plant: Two 4,000 lb (1 814 kg) Rolls-Royce Viper 623 turbojets.
Performance: (Estimated) Max. speed, 700 mph (1 126 km/h) or Mach 0·92 at sea level, 627 mph (1 010 km/h) or Mach 0·95 at 40,000 ft (12 190 m); radius of action with 4,410-lb (2 000-kg) warload (lo-lo-lo), 155 mls (250 km), (hi-lo-hi), 280 mls (450 km); initial climb, 17,700 ft/min (90 m/sec); service ceiling, 44,290 ft (13 500 m).
Weights: (Estimated) Empty equipped, 9,700 lb (4 400 kg); max. take-off, 19,840 lb (9 000 kg).
Armament: Two 30-mm cannon and up to 4,410 lb (2 000 kg) of ordnance on five external stations.
Status: First of three prototypes flown in August 1974. Nine pre-production examples completed during 1976, with first production aircraft scheduled for completion during the first quarter of 1977.
Notes: The Orao (Eagle) has been developed jointly by the Jugoslav and Romanian (JuRom) aircraft industries, being designated by the latter as the IAR 93. The Jugoslav SOKO organisation is airframe team leader and is responsible for final assembly from Jugoslav- and Romanian-manufactured components, and the Viper 623 turbojet is licence-manufactured in Romania.

JUROM (IAR 93) ORAO

Dimensions: (Estimated) Span, 24 ft 7 in (7,50 m); length, 42 ft 8 in (13,00 m); height, 12 ft 1½ in (3,70 m); wing area, 193·75 sq ft (18,00 m²).

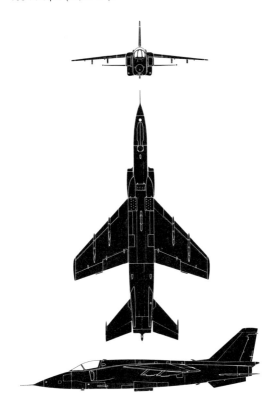

LOCKHEED JETSTAR II

Country of Origin: USA.
Type: Light business executive transport.
Power Plant: Four 3,700 lb (1 678 kg) Garrett AiResearch TFE 731-3 turbofans.
Performance: Max. speed, 552 mph (888 km/h) at 23,000 ft (7 010 m); econ. cruise, 508 mph (817 km/h) at 35,000 ft (10 670 m); range (with max. fuel and 30 min reserves), 3,189 mls (5 132 km), (max. payload and 30 min reserves), 2,994 mls (4 818 km); initial climb, 4,100 ft/min (20,82 m/sec); service ceiling, 38,000 ft (11 580 m).
Weights: Basic operational, 24,178 lb (10 967 kg); max. take-off, 43,750 lb (19 844 kg).
Accommodation: Flight crew of two and normal accommodation for 10 passengers in main cabin.
Status: First production JetStar II flown on August 18, 1976, with first customer delivery following in September. Production rate of 1·5 aircraft monthly at beginning of 1977 with annual production of 18 scheduled through 1978.
Notes: The Model 1329-25 JetStar II is essentially a re-engined version of the earlier JetStar (see 1964 edition), a total of 166 examples of which had been built when deliveries were completed in 1973. In addition to new production of the JetStar II, AiResearch is offering a re-engining scheme to convert earlier JetStars to the new standard, the first AiResearch conversion having flown on July 10, 1974. The replacement of the Pratt & Whitney JT12 turbojets of the original JetStar by TFE 731-3 turbofans offers significant improvements in both range and noise levels, and also allows an increase in maximum take-off weight.

124

LOCKHEED JETSTAR II

Dimensions: Span, 54 ft 5 in (16,60 m); length, 60 ft 5 in (18,42 m); height, 20 ft 5 in (6,23 m); wing area, 542·5 sq ft (50,40 m²).

LOCKHEED L-1011-200 TRISTAR

Country of Origin: USA.

Type: Medium- to long-haul commercial transport.

Power Plant: Three 48,000 lb (21 772 kg) Rolls-Royce RB.211-524 turbofans.

Performance: (At 360,000 lb/163 290 kg) Max. cruise, 608 mph (978 km/h) at 31,000 ft (9 450 m); econ. cruise, 567 mph (913 km/h) at 31,000 ft (9 450 m); long-range cruise, 557 mph (896 km/h); range (at 466,000 lb/211 375 kg) with 74,200-lb (33 657-kg) payload, 4,887 mls (7 865 km), with max. fuel and 42,827-lb (19 426-kg) payload, 6,208 mls (9 992 km).

Weights: Operational empty, 245,800 lb (111 493 kg); max. take-off, 466,000 lb (211 375 kg).

Accommodation: Basic flight crew of three—four. Typical passenger configuration provides 256 seats in a ratio of 20% first class and 80% coach class. All-economy configurations provide for up to 400 passengers.

Status: L-1011-1 first flown November 16, 1970, with first deliveries (to Eastern) following in April 1972. Deliveries of the longer-range L-1011-100 initiated (to Cathay Pacific) August 1975, with the more powerful L-1011-200 to enter service (with Saudia) early 1977. One hundred and thirty-eight TriStars delivered by beginning of 1977.

Notes: Externally identical and complementary to the basic L-1011-1, the L-1011-100 is available with either 42,000 lb (19 050 kg) RB.211-22B or 43,500 lb (19 730 kg) RB.211-22F engines, while the L-1011-200 features additional centre-section fuel tankage and RB.211-524 engines. The long-range L-1011-500 ordered by British Airways (six) on August 6, 1976 will differ from the -200 in having 50,000 lb (22,700 kg) RB-211-524Bs, a 13 ft 6 in (4,11 m) shorter fuselage and a take-off weight of 496,000 lb (224 982 kg).

LOCKHEED L-1011-200 TRISTAR

Dimensions: Span, 155 ft 4 in (47,34 m); length, 178 ft 8 in (54,35 m); height, 55 ft 4 in (16,87 m); wing area, 3,456 sq ft (320,0 m²).

LOCKHEED C-130H HERCULES

Country of Origin: USA.

Type: Medium- to long-range military transport.

Power Plant: Four 4,050 eshp Allison T56-A-7A turbo-props.

Performance: Max. speed, 384 mph (618 km/h); max. cruise, 368 mph (592 km/h); econ. cruise, 340 mph (547 km/h); range (with max. payload and 5% plus 30 min reserves), 2,450 mls (3 943 km); max. range, 4,770 mls (7 675 km); initial climb, 1,900 ft/min (9,65 m/sec).

Weights: Empty equipped, 72,892 lb (33 063 kg); max. normal take-off, 155,000 lb (70 310 kg); max. overload, 175,000 lb (79 380 kg).

Accommodation: Flight crew of four and max. of 92 fully-equipped troops, 64 paratroops, or 74 casualty stretchers and two medical attendants. As a cargo carrier up to six pre-loaded freight pallets may be carried.

Status: The C-130H is the principal current production version of the Hercules which, in progressively developed forms, has been in continuous production since 1952, and at the beginning of 1977, when some 1,440 Hercules had been delivered, production rate was six per month.

Notes: The C-130H, which was in process of delivery to the USAF, Bolivia, Greece, Malaysia, Morocco, Portugal and Saudi Arabia at the beginning of 1977, is basically a C-130E with more powerful engines, and the Hercules C Mk. 1 (C-130K) serving with the RAF differs in having some UK-supplied instruments, avionics and other items. The current production version of the C-130H is known as the "Advanced H" which embodies various refinements.

LOCKHEED C-130H HERCULES

Dimensions: Span, 132 ft 7 in (40,41 m); length, 97 ft 9 in (29,78 m); height, 38 ft 3 in (11,66 m); wing area, 1,745 sq ft (162,12 m²).

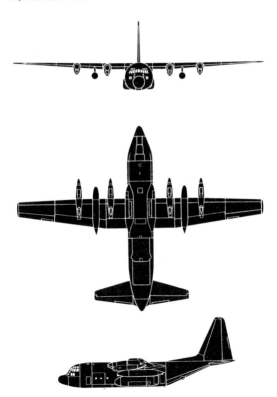

LOCKHEED P-3C ORION

Country of Origin: USA.

Type: Long-range maritime patrol aircraft.

Power Plant: Four 4,910 eshp Allison T56-A-14W turbo-props.

Performance: Max. speed at 105,000 lb (47 625 kg), 473 mph (761 km/h) at 15,000 ft (4 570 m); normal cruise, 397 mph (639 km/h) at 25,000 ft (7 620 ml); patrol speed, 230 mph (370 km/h) at 1,500 ft (457 m); loiter endurance (all engines) at 1,500 ft (457 m) 12·3 hours, (two engines), 17 hrs; max. mission radius, 2,530 mls (4 075 km), with 3 hrs on station at 1,500 ft (457 m), 1,933 mls (3 110 km); initial climb, 2,880 ft/min (14,6 m/sec).

Weights: Empty, 61,491 lb (27 890 kg); normal max. take-off, 133,500 lb (60 558 kg); max. overload, 142,000 lb (64 410 kg).

Accommodation: Normal flight crew of 10 of which five housed in tactical compartment. Up to 50 combat troops and 4,000 lb (1 814 kg) of equipment for trooping role.

Armament: Weapons bay can house two Mk 101 depth bombs and four Mk 43, 44 or 46 torpedoes, or eight Mk 54 bombs. External ordnance load of up to 13,713 lb (6 220 kg).

Status: YP-3C prototype flown October 8, 1968, P-3C deliveries commencing to US Navy mid-1969 with approx. 120 delivered by 1977, and at least 12 aircraft per year to be ordered until 1985.

Notes: The P-3C differs from the P-3A (157 built) and -3B (145 built) primarily in having more advanced sensor equipment. Twelve P-3As have been modified as EP-3Es for the electronic reconnaissance role. Six Orions have been delivered to Iran as P-3Fs, 10 P-3Cs are to be delivered to the RAAF from 1977, and 18 are to be delivered to Canada as CP-140 Auroras from 1980.

LOCKHEED P-3C ORION

Dimensions: Span, 99 ft 8 in (30,37 m); length, 116 ft 10 in (35,61 m); height, 33 ft 8½ in (10,29 m); wing area, 1,300 sq ft (120,77 m²).

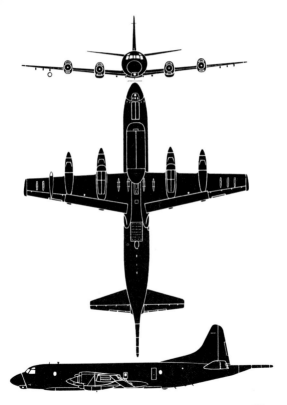

LOCKHEED S-3A VIKING

Country of Origin: USA.

Type: Four-seat shipboard anti-submarine aircraft.

Power Plant: Two 9,280 lb (4 210 kg) General Electric TF34-GE-2 turbofans.

Performance: Max. speed, 506 mph (815 km/h) at sea level; max. cruise, 403 mph (649 km/h); typical loiter speed, 184 mph (257 km/h); max. ferry range, 3,500 mls (5 630 km) plus; initial climb, 3,937 ft/min (20 m/sec); service ceiling, 35,000 ft (10 670 m); sea level endurance, 7·5 hrs at 186 mph (300 km/h).

Weights: Empty equipped, 26,554 lb (12 044 kg); normal max. take-off, 43,491 lb (19 727 kg).

Accommodation: Pilot and co-pilot side by side on flight deck, with tactical co-ordinator and sensor operator in aft cabin. All four crew members provided with zero-zero ejection seats.

Armament: Various combinations of torpedoes, depth charges, bombs and ASMs in internal weapons bay and on underwing pylons.

Status: First of eight development and evaluation aircraft commenced its test programme on January 21, 1972, and remaining seven had flown by early 1973. Current US Navy acquisition of 184 production aircraft to be completed during 1977.

Notes: Intended as a successor to the Grumman S-2 Tracker in US Navy service, Lockheed's shipboard turbofan-powered ASW aircraft was selected for development mid-1969, and entered fleet service during the course of 1974.

LOCKHEED S-3A VIKING

Dimensions: Span, 68 ft 8 in (20,93 m); length, 53 ft 4 in (16,26 m); height, 22 ft 9 in (6,93 m); wing area, 598 sq ft (55,56 m²).

LTV AEROSPACE A-7E CORSAIR II

Country of Origin: USA.

Type: Single-seat shipboard tactical fighter.

Power Plant: One 15,000 lb (6 804 kg) Allison TF41-A-2 (Rolls-Royce RB. 168-62 Spey) turbofan.

Performance: Max. speed without external stores, 699 mph (1 125 km/h) or Mach 0·92 at sea level, with 12 250-lb (113,4-kg) bombs, 633 mph (1 020 km/h) or Mach 0·87 at sea level; tactical radius with 12 250-lb (113,4-kg) bombs for hi-lo-hi mission at average cruise of 532 mph (856 km/h) with 1 hr on station, 512 mls (825 km); ferry range on internal fuel, 2,775 mls (4 465 km).

Weights: Empty equipped, 17,569 lb (7 969 kg); max. take-off, 42,000+ lb (19 050+ kg).

Armament: One 20-mm M-61A-1 rotary cannon with 1,000 rounds and (for short-range interdiction) maximum ordnance load of 20,000 lb (9 072 kg).

Status: A-7E first flown November 25, 1968, with production deliveries to US Navy following mid-1969. First 67 delivered with Pratt & Whitney TF30-P-8 (subsequently re-designated A-7Cs). Planned procurement totals 706 aircraft with final deliveries in 1981.

Notes: A-7E is the shipboard equivalent of the USAF's A-7D (see 1970 edition). Preceded into service by A-7A (199 built) and A-7B (196 built) with 11.350 lb (5 150 kg) TF30-P-6 and 12,200 lb (5 534 kg) TF30-P-8 respectively. Eighty-one early Corsairs (40 A-7Bs and 41 A-7Cs) are being converted as tandem two-seat TA-7Cs for 1977–78 delivery in the training role. Delivery of 60 A-7Hs (equivalent to A-7D) to Greece to be completed in 1977.

LTV AEROSPACE A-7E CORSAIR II

Dimensions: Span, 38 ft $8\frac{3}{4}$ in (11,80 m); length, 46 ft $1\frac{1}{2}$ in (14,06 m); height, 16 ft $0\frac{3}{4}$ in (4,90 m); wing area, 375 sq ft (34,83 m²).

McDONNELL DOUGLAS DC-9 SERIES 50

Country of Origin: USA.

Type: Short-to-medium-haul commercial transport.

Power Plant: Two 16,000 lb (7 257 kg) Pratt & Whitney JT8D-17 turbofans.

Performance: Max. cruise, 564 mph (907 km/h) at 27,000 ft (8 230 m); econ. cruise, 535 mph (861 km/h) at 33,000 ft (10 060 m); long-range cruise, 509 mph (819 km/h) at 35,000 ft (10 668 m); range with max. payload (33,000 lb/ 14 950 kg), 1,468 mls (2 362 km), with max. fuel (and 21,400-lb/9 700-kg payload), 2,787 mls (4 485 km).

Weights: Operational empty, 65,000 lb (29 484 kg); max. take-off, 120,000 lb (54 430 kg).

Accommodation: Flight crew of two/three and maximum high-density arrangement for 139 passengers in five-abreast seating.

Status: The first DC-9 Series 50 flew on December 17, 1974, with first delivery (against initial order for 10 from Swissair) following during July 1975. Fifty-six firm orders for the Series 50 had been received by the beginning of 1977, when total orders for all versions of the DC-9 were 865 aircraft.

Notes: The latest of five basic DC-9 models, the Series 50 represents a further "stretch" of the basic DC-9 airframe, the fuselage being 6·4 ft (1,95 m) longer than the previously largest DC-9, the Series 40. The DC-9 was first flown on February 25, 1965, and the 700th aircraft of this type was delivered in July 1973. Production versions include the initial Series 10, the Series 20 (see 1969 edition) retaining the short fuselage of the Series 10 with the longer-span wing of the Series 30 (see 1973 edition) and the Series 40 (see 1972 edition). The DC-9QSF (Quiet, Short Field) was being offered in 1976 with an enlarged wing and refanned engines.

McDONNELL DOUGLAS DC-9 SERIES 50

Dimensions: Span, 93 ft 5 in (28,47 m); length, 132 ft 0 in (40,23 m); height, 27 ft 6 in (8,38 m); wing area, 1,000·7 sq ft (92,97 m²).

McDONNELL DOUGLAS DC-10 SERIES 30

Country of Origin: USA.

Type: Medium-range commercial transport.

Power Plant: Three 51,000 lb (23 134 kg) General Electric CF6-50C turbofans.

Performance: Max. cruise (at 520,000 lb/235 868 kg), 570 mph (917 km/h) at 31,000 ft (9 450 m); long-range cruise, 554 mph (891 km/h) at 31,000 ft (9 450 m); max. fuel range (with 230 mls/370 km reserves), 6,909 mls (11 118 km); max. payload range, 4,272 mls (6 875 km); max. climb rate, 2,320 ft/min (11,78 m/sec); service ceiling (at 540,000 lb/244 940 kg), 32,700 ft (9 965 m).

Weights: Basic operating, 263,087 lb (119 334 kg); max. take-off, 555,000 lb (251 745 kg).

Accommodation: Flight crew of three plus provision on flight deck for two supernumerary crew. Typical mixed-class accommodation for 225–270 passengers. Max. authorised passenger accommodation, 380 (plus crew of 11).

Status: First DC-10 (Series 10) flown August 29, 1970, with first Series 30 (46th DC-10 built) flying June 21, 1972, being preceded on February 28, 1972, by first Series 40. Orders totalled 246 by the beginning of 1977.

Notes: The DC-10 Series 30 and 40 have identical fuselages to the DC-10 Series 10 (see 1972 edition), but whereas the last-mentioned version is a domestic model, the Series 30 and 40 are intercontinental models, and differ in power plant, weight and wing details, and in the use of three main undercarriage units, the third (a twin-wheel unit) being mounted on the fuselage centreline. The Series 40 has 49,400 lb (22 407 kg) Pratt & Whitney JT9D-20 turbofans but is otherwise similar to the Series 30.

138

McDONNELL DOUGLAS DC-10 SERIES 30

Dimensions: Span, 165 ft 4 in (50,42 m); length, 181 ft 4$\frac{3}{4}$ in (55,29 m); height, 58 ft 0 in (17,68 m); wing area, 3,921·4 sq ft (364,3 m²).

McDONNELL DOUGLAS F-4E PHANTOM

Country of Origin: USA.

Type: Two-seat interceptor and tactical strike fighter.

Power Plant: Two 11,870 lb (5 385 kg) dry and 17,900 lb (8 120 kg) reheat General Electric J79-GE-17 turbojets.

Performance: Max. speed without external stores, 910 mph (1 464 km/h) or Mach 1·2 at 1,000 ft (305 m), 1,500 mph (2 414 km/h) or Mach 2·27 at 40,000 ft (12 190 m); tactical radius (with four Sparrow III and four Sidewinder AAMs), 140 mls (225 km), (plus one 500 Imp gal/2 273 l auxiliary tank), 196 mls (315 km), (hi-lo-hi mission profile with four 1,000-lb/453,6-kg bombs, four AAMs, and one 500 Imp gal/2 273 l and two 308 Imp gal/1,400 l tanks), 656 mls (1 056 km); max. ferry range, 2,300 mls (3 700 km) at 575 mph (925 km/h).

Weights: Empty equipped, 30,425 lb (13 801 kg); loaded (with four Sparrow IIIs), 51,810 lb (21 500 kg), (plus four Sidewinders and max. external fuel), 58,000 lb (26 308 kg); max. overload, 60,630 lb (27 502 kg).

Armament: One 20-mm M-61A1 rotary cannon and (intercept) four or six AIM-7E plus four AIM-9D AAMs, or (attack) up to 16,000 lb (7 257 kg) of external stores.

Status: First F-4E flown June 1967, and production continuing at beginning of 1974. Some 4,850 Phantoms (all versions) delivered by beginning of 1977, with 5,000th scheduled for mid-1977 delivery.

Notes: Current production models of the Phantom in addition to the F-4E are the RF-4E (see 1972 edition) and the F-4EJ for Japan. The F-4F for Federal Germany, optimised for the intercept role with simplified avionics, entered service with the Luftwaffe from January 1, 1974, and features leading-edge slats and various weight-saving features, the slats now being standardised by the F-4E. The last of 175 F-4Fs was delivered to the Luftwaffe in April 1976.

McDONNELL DOUGLAS F-4E PHANTOM

Dimensions: Span, 38 ft 4¾ in (11,70 m); length, 62 ft 10½ in (19,20 m); height, 16 ft 3⅓ in (4,96 m); wing area, 530 sq ft (49,2 m²).

McDONNELL DOUGLAS F-15 EAGLE

Country of Origin: USA.

Type: Single-seat air superiority fighter (F-15A) and two-seat operational trainer (TF-15A).

Power Plant: Two (approx.) 25,000 lb (11 340 kg) reheat Pratt & Whitney F100-PW-100 turbofans.

Performance: Max. speed, 915 mph (1 472 km/h) at sea level or Mach 1·2, 1,650 mph (2 655 km/h) at 36,090 ft (11 000 m) or Mach 2·5; tactical radius (combat air patrol), up to 1,120 mls (1 800 km); ferry range, 2,980 mls (4 800 km), (with Fast Pack auxiliary tanks), 3,450 mls (5 560 km).

Weights: Empty equipped, 26,147 lb (11 860 kg); loaded (clean), 38,250 lb (17 350 kg); max. take-off (intercept mission), 40,000 lb (18 145 kg); max. take-off, 54,123 lb (24 550 kg).

Armament: One 20-mm M-61A-1 rotary cannon with 950 rounds and (intercept mission) four AIM-9L Sidewinder and four AIM-7F Sparrow AAMs. Five stores stations (four wing and one fuselage) can lift up to 15,000 lb (6 804 kg) of ordnance.

Status: Twenty test and development aircraft ordered (18 F-15As and two TF-15As) with first F-15A flying on July 27, 1972, and first TF-15A on July 7, 1973. Current planning calls for acquisition of 729 Eagles by USAF, every seventh aircraft being a TF-15A, and the 150th production aircraft was scheduled for delivery during January 1977, when production rate was nine per month.

Notes: The Eagle is to equip 19 USAF squadrons, deliveries of 25 to Israel commenced on December 10, 1976, and the Eagle has been selected by Japan's Air Self-Defence Force for service introduction from the beginning of the 'eighties.

McDONNELL DOUGLAS F-15 EAGLE

Dimensions: Span, 42 ft 9¾ in (13,05 m); length, 63 ft 9 in (19,43 m); height, 18 ft 5½ in (5,63 m); wing area, 608 sq ft (56,50 m²).

McDONNELL DOUGLAS A-4N SKYHAWK II

Country of Origin: USA.

Type: Single-seat light attack bomber.

Power Plant: One 11,200 lb (5 080 kg) Pratt & Whitney J52-P-408A turbojet.

Performance: Max. speed without external stores, 685 mph (1 102 km/h) or Mach 0·9 at sea level, 640 mph (1 030 km/h) at 25,000 ft (7 620 m), in high drag configuration, 625 mph (1 080 km/h) or Mach 0·82 at sea level, 605 mph (973 km/h) or Mach 0·84 at 30,000 ft (9 145 m); combat radius on internal fuel for hi-lo-lo-hi mission profile with 4,000 lb (1 814 kg) of external stores, 340 mls (547 km); initial climb, 15,850 ft/min (80,5 m/sec), at 23,000 lb (10 433 kg), 8,440 ft/min (42,7 m/sec).

Weights: Empty, 10,600 lb (4 808 kg); max. take-off, 24,500 lb (11 113 kg).

Armament: Two 30-mm DEFA cannon and external weapons loads up to 8,200 lb (3 720 kg) under wing and fuselage.

Status: First A-4N flown June 12, 1972, with first production deliveries (to Israel) initiated November 1972. Production of similar A-4M continuing into 1977.

Notes: The A-4N employs essentially the same power plant and airframe as the A-4M (illustrated above), both models being referred to as the Skyhawk II. The A-4N embodies some of the features originally developed for the Israeli A-4H (e.g., twin 30-mm cannon) but has a new nav/attack system and revised cockpit. Thirty-six A-4M Skyhawks are to be delivered to Kuwait during 1977. All USMC A-4Ms are to be updated as A-4Ys with redesigned cockpit and revised systems.

McDONNELL DOUGLAS A-4N SKYHAWK II

Dimensions: Span, 27 ft 6 in (8,38 m); length, 40 ft 3¼ in (12,27 m); height, 15 ft 0 in (4,57 m); wing area, 260 sq ft (24,16 m²).

McDONNELL DOUGLAS YC-15

Country of Origin: USA.

Type: Medium STOL tactical transport.

Power Plant: Four 16,000 lb (7 258 kg) Pratt & Whitney JT8D-17 turbofans.

Performance: (Estimated) Max. speed, 535 mph (861 km/h); operational radius utilising STOL techniques with 27,000-lb (12 247-kg) payload or conventional techniques with 62,000-lb (28 122-kg) payload, 460 mls (740 km); ferry range, 2,992 mls (4 814 km).

Weights: Max. take-off, 216,680 lb (98 286 kg).

Accommodation: Flight crew of three. Hold can accommodate all US Army vehicles up to and including the 62,000-lb (28 123-kg) extended-barrel self-propelled 8-in (20,3-cm) howitzer. Approximately 150 fully-equipped troops may be carried or mix of troops and freight (eg, six freight pallets and 40 troops).

Status: First YC-15 flown August 26, 1975, with second following on December 5, 1975. The YC-15 is participating in a prototype fly-off contest with the Boeing YC-14 (see pages 42–43), with production decision expected by September 1977.

Notes: McDonnell Douglas's contender for the USAF's advanced military STOL transport (AMST) requirement, the YC-15 derives short take-off and landing characteristics from a variety of high-lift devices, including double-slotted flaps over some 75% of the total wing span and operating directly in the exhaust stream from the widely-spaced turbofans. The YC-15 can operate into and out of 2,000-ft (610-m) runways.

And

McDONNELL DOUGLAS YC-15

Dimensions: Span, 110 ft 4 in (33,64 m); length, 124 ft 3 in (37,90 m); height, 43 ft 4 in (13,20 m); wing area, 1,740 sq ft (161,65 m²).

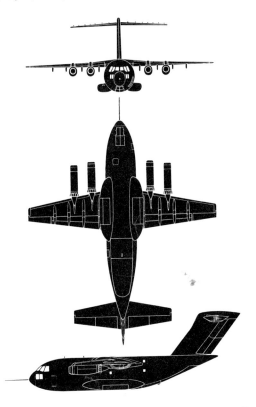

MIKOYAN MIG-23S (FLOGGER-B)

Country of Origin: USSR.

Type: Single-seat interceptor and air superiority fighter (and two-seat conversion trainer—Flogger-C).

Power Plant: One (estimated) 14,330 lb (6 500 kg) dry and 23,150 lb (10 500 kg) reheat Tumansky turbofan.

Performance: (Estimated) Max. speed, 865 mph (1 392 km/h) at 1,000 ft (305 m) or Mach 1·2, 1,520 mph (2 446 km/h) above 39,370 ft (12 000 m) or Mach 2·3; combat radius (intercept mission), 450 mls (725 km); normal max. range, 1,400 mls (2 250 km); ferry range (three 330 Imp gal/1 500 l external tanks), 2,485 mls (4 000 km) at 495 mph (796 km/h) or Mach 0·75.

Weights: (Estimated) Empty equipped, 18,000 lb (8 165 kg); normal loaded, 34,600 lb (15 700 kg); max. take-off, 39,130 lb (17 750 kg).

Armament: One 23-mm twin-barrel GSh-23 cannon plus two AA-7 Apex and two AA-8 Aphid AAMs.

Status: The MiG-23S reportedly entered service in the intercept and air superiority roles with the Soviet Air Forces in 1971, and upwards of 1,000 fighters of this type were believed to be in Soviet service by the beginning of 1977.

Notes: The MiG-23S, together with a tandem two-seat operational training variant, the MiG-23U (Flogger-C), had been exported to Egypt, Iraq, Libya and Syria, and has a 90-cm diameter (High Lark) radar. Development of the basic design for the battlefield interdiction role resulted in the MiG-27 (Flogger-D) described and illustrated on pages 152–153.

MIKOYAN MIG-23S (FLOGGER-B)

Dimensions: (Estimated) Span (max.), 46 ft 9 in (14,25 m), (min.), 27 ft 6 in (8,38 m); length (including probe), 55 ft 1½ in (16,80 m); wing area, 293·4 sq ft (27,26 m²).

MIKOYAN MIG-25 (FOXBAT)

Country of Origin: USSR.

Type: Single-seat interceptor fighter (Foxbat-A) and high-altitude reconnaissance aircraft (Foxbat-B).

Power Plant: Two (estimated) 17,640 lb (8 000 kg) dry and 24,250 lb (11 000 kg) reheat Tumansky turbojets.

Performance: (Estimated—Foxbat-A) Max. short-period dash speed, 1,850 mph (2 980 km/h) or Mach 2·8 above 36,000 ft (10 970 m); max. sea level speed, 650 mph (1 045 km/h) or Mach 0·85; mission radius (max. internal fuel), 590 mls (950 km); max. range, 1,240 mls (2 000 km); service ceiling, 72,180 ft (22 000 m).

Weights: Empty, 44,100 lb (20 000 kg); max. take-off, 77,160 lb (35 000 kg).

Armament: Four AA-6 Acrid AAMs (two infra-red homing and two semi-active radar homing).

Status: The MiG-25 commenced its development trials in the mid 'sixties and apparently entered service in the high-altitude intercept role in 1970–71, and in the reconnaissance role in 1972. In excess of 400 MiG-25s were estimated to be in service by the beginning of 1977.

Notes: Two operational versions of the MiG-25 are known to exist: a missile-armed high-altitude interceptor and a reconnaissance model (illustrated above) in which the Fox Fire intercept radar is replaced by a battery of cameras, the latter version being Foxbat-B. A conversion training version with a second cockpit in the forward fuselage (Foxbat-C) possesses no operational capability.

MIKOYAN MIG-25 (FOXBAT)

Dimensions: Span, 45 ft 11 in (14,00 m); length (including probe), 73 ft 2 in (22,30 m); height, 18 ft 4½ in (5,60 m); wing area, 602·78 sq ft (56,00 m²).

MIKOYAN MIG-27 (FLOGGER-D)

Country of Origin: USSR.

Type: Single-seat tactical strike fighter.

Power Plant: One (estimated) 15,500 lb (7 025 kg) dry and 20,500 lb (9 300 kg) reheat Tumansky turbofan.

Performance: (Estimated) Max. speed, 865 mph (1 392 km/h) at 1,000 ft (305 m) or Mach 1·2, 990 mph (1 590 km/h) above 39,370 ft (12 000 m) or Mach 1·5; combat radius (hi-lo-hi with centreline drop tank), 620 mls (1 000 km), (lo-lo-lo), 220 mls (350 km); normal max. range, 1,550 mls (2 500 km); ferry range (three 330 Imp gal/1 500 l drop tanks), 2,610 mls (4 200 km).

Weights: (Estimated) Empty equipped, 18,000 lb (8 165 kg); normal loaded, 35,275 lb (16 000 kg).

Armament: One 23-mm six-barrel rotary cannon and up to four AS-7 Kerry ASMs or various bombs up to 6,600 lb (total) on five external stations.

Status: A derivative of the MiG-23 interceptor, the MiG-27 is believed to have entered service with the Soviet Air Forces in 1974, and is now numerically one of the most important types deployed with the Forces Groups along the Soviet western periphery.

Notes: The MiG-27 differs from the MiG-23S (see pages 148–149) in having simple fixed engine air intakes in place of variable-area intakes, a simpler, shorter exhaust nozzle for lower-boost reheat, a redesigned nose with laser range, a sturdier undercarriage with low-pressure tyres and bulged housings, and repositioned weapon pylons. The MiG-27 is optimised for the battlefield interdiction and counterair roles.

MIKOYAN MIG-27 (FLOGGER-D)

Dimensions: (Estimated) Span (max.), 46 ft 9 in (14,25 m), (min.), 27 ft 6 in (8,38 m); length (including probe), 54 ft 0 in (16,46 m); wing area, 293·4 sq ft (27,26 m²).

MITSUBISHI F-1

Country of Origin: Japan.

Type: Single-seat ground attack aircraft.

Power Plant: Two 3,820 lb (1 730 kg) and 7,070 lb (3 210 kg) reheat Ishikawajima-Harima TF40-IHI-801A (Rolls-Royce/Turboméca RB.172-T.260 Adour) turbofans.

Performance: Max. speed, 1,056 mph (1 700 km/h) at 40,000 ft (12 190 m) or Mach 1·6; combat radius (hi-lo-hi) with 500-lb (226,8-kg) bombs, 345 mls (555 km); max. ferry range, 1,785 mls (2 870 km); time to 36,090 ft (11 000 m), 2·0 min.

Weights: Empty equipped, 14,330 lb (6 500 kg); max. take-off, 30,200 lb (13 700 kg).

Armament: One 20-mm multi-barrel Vulcan M61A-1 cannon and up to 8,000 lb (3 629 kg) of stores on seven external stations (one under fuselage and six under wings). Two infra-red homing AAMs may be mounted at wingtips. Typical load comprises eight 500-lb (226,8-kg) bombs plus two 183 Imp gal (832 l) fuel tanks. Primary armament to be two Mitsubishi ASM-1 anti-shipping missiles.

Status: First prototype flown (as FS-T2 kai) on June 7, 1975, having been preceded by second prototype on June 3, these having been adapted from the 6th and 7th production T-2A trainers. Twenty-six F-1s ordered by beginning of 1977, with purchase of further 37 planned. First of three F-1 squadrons scheduled to be formed March 1978.

Notes: The F-1 is a single-seat ground attack variant of the T-2A tandem two-seat advanced trainer (see 1975 edition) of which 63 have been ordered by the Japanese Air Self-Defence Force. The F-1 has two additional wing hardpoints, a new fire control system and numerous other changes, and it is anticipated that the first production F-1 will be completed in April 1977.

MITSUBISHI F-1

Dimensions: Span, 25 ft 10 in (7,87 m); length, 58 ft 7 in (17,86 m); height, 14 ft 7 in (4,44 m); wing area, 228 sq ft (21,18 m²).

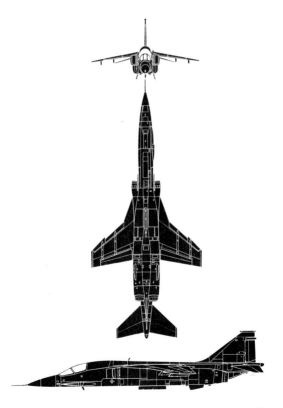

MUDRY CAP 20L

Country of Origin: France.

Type: Single-seat aerobatic competition aircraft.

Power Plant: One (CAP 20L-180) 180 hp Avco Lycoming IO-360-RCF or (CAP 20L-200L) 200 hp AIO-360-B1B four-cylinder horizontally-opposed engine.

Performance: (CAP 20L-180) Max. speed, 176 mph (283 km/h) at sea level; max. cruise, 168 mph (270 km/h) at sea level; initial climb, 2,560 ft/min (13 m/sec); (CAP 20L-200) max. cruise, 168 mph (270 km/h); initial climb, 2,953 ft/min (15 m/sec).

Weights: (CAP 20L-180) Empty, 1,014 lb (460 kg); max. take-off (Cat. A), 1,322 lb (600 kg); (CAP 20L-200) Empty, 1,058 lb (480 kg); max. take-off (Cat. A), 1,367 lb (620 kg).

Status: The prototype (CAP 20L-180) was first flown on January 15, 1976, and the first of a pre-series of five aircraft was flown in October 1976. Certification was anticipated for January 1977.

Notes: The CAP 20L (*léger*) is a lightweight development of the CAP 20 (which, in turn, was a single-seat derivative of the side-by-side two-seat CAP 10) which flew as a prototype on July 29, 1969, and was subsequently produced as the CAP 20A for the *Equipe de Voltige Aerienne* of the *Armée de l'Air*. Both the CAP 20L-180 and -200 have fixed-pitch propellers, but proposed versions include the CAP 20LS-180 and -200 with Hartzell or Hoffman variable-pitch propellers, and the CAP 20LS-260 with a 260 hp six-cylinder Avco Lycoming AEIO-540-D4B5 engine.

MUDRY CAP 20L

Dimensions: Span, 24 ft 4½ in (7,43 m); length, 23 ft 1½ in (7,05 m); height, 8 ft 4½ in (2,55 m); wing area, 111·9 sq ft (10,40 m²).

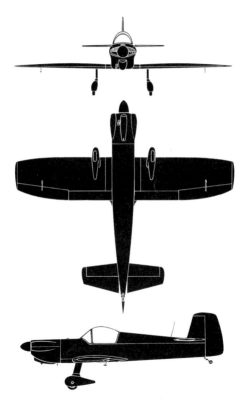

NORTHROP F-5E TIGER II

Country of Origin: USA.

Type: Single-seat air-superiority fighter.

Power Plant: Two 3,500 lb (1 588 kg) dry and 5,000 lb (2 268 kg) reheat General Electric J85-GE-21 turbojets.

Performance: Max. speed (at 13,220 lb/5 997 kg), 1056 mph (1 700 km/h) or Mach 1·6 at 36,090 ft (11 000 m), 760 mph (1 223 km/h) or Mach 1·0 at sea level, (with wingtip missiles), 990 mph (1 594 km/h) or Mach 1·5 at 36,090 ft (11 000 m); combat radius (internal fuel), 173 mls (278 km), (with 229 Imp gal/1 041 l drop tank), 426 mls (686 km); initial climb (at 13,220 lb/5 997 kg), 31,600 ft/min (160,53 m/sec); combat ceiling, 53,500 ft (16 305 m).

Weights: Take-off (wingtip launching rail configuration), 15,400 lb (6 985 kg); max. take-off, 24,083 lb (10 924 kg).

Armament: Two 20-mm M-39 cannon with 280 rpg and two wingtip-mounted AIM-9 Sidewinder AAMs. Up to 7,000 lb (3 175 kg) of ordnance (for attack role).

Status: First F-5E flown August 11, 1972, and first deliveries February 1973. Forty-eight delivered during 1973, followed by 158 in 1974, and production attaining 15 per month in 1975, at which (including F-5F) it was running at the beginning of 1977.

Notes: A more powerful derivative of the F-5A (see 1970 edition) optimised for the air-superiority role, the F-5E won the USAF's International Fighter Aircraft (IFA) contest in November 1970, and is being supplied under the Military Assistance Programme to South Korea, Taiwan, Thailand and Jordan. Orders for the F-5E have also been placed by eight other air forces, small numbers having also been supplied to the USAF and US Navy. The first two-seat F-5F flew on September 25, 1974, and production deliveries of this version began mid-1976. The F-5E may be fitted with a camera nose.

NORTHROP F-5E TIGER II

Dimensions: Span, 26 ft 8½ in (8,14 m); length, 48 ft 2½ in (14,69 m); height, 13 ft 4 in (4,06 m); wing area, 186·2 sq ft (17,29 m²).

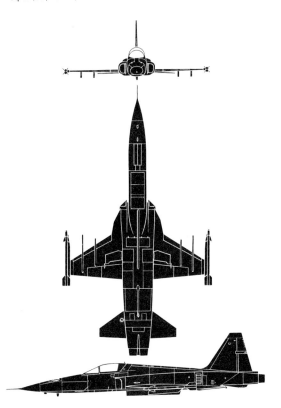

PANAVIA TORNADO

Countries of Origin: UK, Federal Germany and Italy.
Type: Two-seat multi-role fighter.
Power Plant: Two 8,500 lb (3 855 kg) dry and 15,000 lb (6 800 kg) reheat Turbo-Union RB.199-34R-4 Mk 101 turbofans.
Performance: (Estimated) Max. speed (clean), 840 mph (1 350 km/h) at 500 ft (150 m) or Mach 1·1, 1,385 mph (2 230 km/h) at 36,090 ft (11 000 m) or Mach 2·1; tactical radius (lo-lo-lo) with external stores, 450 mls (725 km), (hi-lo-hi) with external stores, 750 mls (1 200 km); max. ferry range, 3,000+ mls (4 830+ km).
Weights: (Estimated) Empty, 28,000 lb (12 700 kg); loaded (clean), 40,000 lb (18 145 kg); max. take-off, 55,000 lb (25 000 kg).
Armament: Two 27-mm Mauser cannon with 125 rpg and various ordnance combinations on seven (three fixed and four swivelling) external stores stations. Possible weapons include Martel and Kormoran ASMs, 1,000-lb (454-kg) Mk 83 and similar bombs, 600-lb (272-kg) cluster bombs, etc.
Status: First of nine prototypes flown on August 14, 1974, and eight flown (four in UK, three in Germany and one in Italy) by beginning of 1977, with six pre-production aircraft scheduled to fly during course of year. First true production Tornado to fly 1978 and current planning calling for acquisition of 385 by the RAF (including 165 of air defence version from 1983), 210 for the *Luftwaffe*, 112 for the *Marineflieger* and 100 for the Italian *Aeronautica Militare*.
Notes: Initial Tornado production will be concentrated on the IDS (interdictor strike) version for all three participating countries, this being followed by the ADV (air defence version) for the RAF which will have some 80% commonality with the basic aircraft, uprated engines, new radar and a new weapon fit.

PANAVIA TORNADO

Dimensions: Span (max.), 45 ft 8 in (13,90 m), (min.), 28 ft 3 in (8,60 m); length, 54 ft 9½ in (16,70 m); height, 18 ft 8½ in (5,70 m); wing area, 322·9 sq ft (30,00 m²).

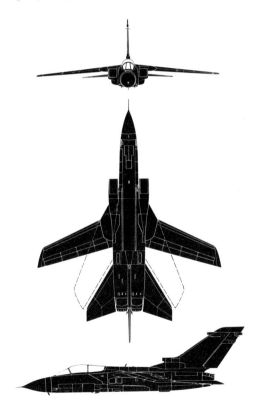

PILATUS PC-7 TURBO TRAINER

Country of Origin: Switzerland.
Type: Tandem two-seat primary and basic trainer.
Power Plant: One 550 shp Pratt & Whitney (Canada) PT6A-25 turboprop.
Performance: Max. speed, 248 mph (400 km/h) at sea level, 270 mph (435 km/h) at 16,405 ft (5 000 m); long-range cruise (60% power), 186 mph (300 km/h) at sea level, 193 mph (310 km/h) at 16,405 ft (5 000 m); max. range (60% power and 20 min but 5% reserves), 683 mls (1 100 km); initial climb (at 4,189 lb/1 900 kg), 2,066 ft/min (10,5 m/sec); service ceiling (at 4,189 lb/1 900 kg), 31,170 ft (9 500 m).
Weights: Empty, 2,822 lb (1 280 kg); loaded (aerobatics), 4,189 lb (1 900 kg); max. take-off, 5,952 lb (2 700 kg).
Armament: Provision for six multi-purpose underwing hardpoints, two inboard of 551-lb (250-kg) and four outboard of 298-lb (135-kg) capacity. Typical loads include four 6×68-mm Matra rocket launchers and two SUU-11B/A 7,62-mm multi-barrel gun pods or twin 7,62-mm Matra gun pods.
Status: First PC-7 prototype flown on April 12, 1966, with second and definitive prototype flying May 1975. Pre-production batch of 10 to be started during 1977, with first deliveries scheduled for first half of 1978.
Notes: The PC-7 is a derivative of the piston-engined PC-3 with revised structure and fuel system, and various aerodynamic refinements.

PILATUS PC-7 TURBO TRAINER

Dimensions: Span, 34 ft $1\frac{1}{2}$ in (10,40 m); length, 31 ft $11\frac{9}{10}$ in (9,75 m); height, 10 ft $6\frac{1}{3}$ in (3,21 m); wing area, 178·68 sq ft (16,60 m²).

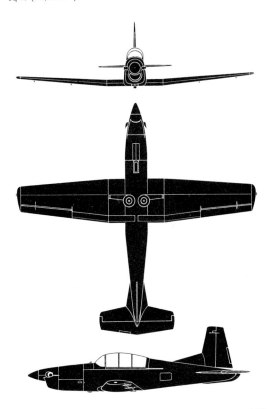

PZL-106A KRUK

Country of Origin: Poland.

Type: Single-seat agricultural aircraft.

Power Plant: One 600 hp PZL-3S seven-cylinder radial air-cooled engine.

Performance: (At 6,170 lb/2 800 kg) Max. speed, 124 mph (200 km/h) at 6,560 ft (2 000 m); max. cruise, 119 mph (180 km/h); normal operating speed, 75–100 mph (120–160 km/h); initial climb rate, 825 ft/min (4,2 m/sec); range, 280 mls (450 km); ferry range (fuel in hopper), 1,120 mls (1 800 km).

Weights: Empty, 3,525 lb (1 600 kg); normal operating, 6,170 lb (2 800 kg); max. take-off, 6,610 lb (3 000 kg).

Status: First prototype flown on April 17, 1973, the second and third prototypes flying in October 1973 and October 1974 respectively. Production initiated during 1976, with first production deliveries scheduled for early 1977. Some 600 are expected to be built for countries of the Council for Mutual Economic Aid.

Notes: The production Kruk (Raven) illustrated on the opposite page differs in a number of respects from the prototypes, the third of which is illustrated above. It features a glass-fibre reinforced plastic hopper/tank ahead of the cockpit and can carry up to 2,200 lb (1 000 kg) of dry or liquid chemicals.

PZL-106A KRUK

Dimensions: Span, 48 ft 6 in (14,80 m); length, 29 ft 2 in (8,90 m); height, 11 ft 10 in (3,60 m); wing area, 305·7 sq ft (28,4 m²).

RFB FANLINER

Country of Origin: Federal Germany.

Type: Light cabin monoplane.

Power Plant: One 150 hp Audi-NSU Wankel KM 871 rotating-piston engine driving a ducted fan.

Performance: Max. cruising speed, 155 mph (250 km/h); initial climb, 1,080 ft/min (5,5 m/sec); range, 620 mls (1 000 km); endurance, 6·5 hrs.

Weights: Empty, 1,200 lb (545 kg); max. take-off, 1,875 lb (850 kg).

Accommodation: Two semi-reclined seats side-by-side with dual controls beneath individual canopies hinged on centreline. Baggage space aft of seats.

Status: First of two production prototypes flown on September 4, 1976, preceded by lower-powered configurational prototype to test propulsion system and first flown on October 8, 1973. Series production expected to commence 1978 and divided between RFB and Grumman (wing and horizontal tail) on two assembly lines, final assembly being divided 20% and 80% between the respective companies.

Notes: The Fanliner utilises a ducted propeller driven by a rotary piston engine, this propulsion system offering lower internal and external noise levels than a conventional propeller installation. Optimum ergonometrical cockpit design is claimed and the Fanliner employs the wing of the Grumman American Traveler, the US company collaborating with RFB in the development and production programme.

RFB FANLINER

Dimensions: Span, 31 ft 6 in (9,6 m); length, 21 ft 8 in (6,59 m); height, 7 ft 5 in (2,27 m); wing area, 139·9 sq ft (13,0 m²).

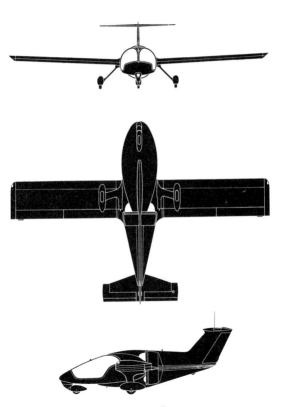

RFB FANTRAINER AWI-2

Country of Origin: Federal Germany.

Type: Tandem two-seat basic trainer.

Power Plant: Two 150 hp Audi-NSU Wankel EA 871-L rotating piston engines driving a ducted fan.

Performance: (Estimated) Max. speed, 220 mph (354 km/h) at sea level, 196 mph (315 km/h) at 20,000 ft (6 095 m); max. range (no reserves), 1,610 mls (2 590 km) at 20,000 ft (6 095 m); initial climb, 1,450 ft/min (7,36 m/sec).

Weights: Operational empty, 2,017 lb (915 kg); max. take-off, 2,976 lb (1 350 kg).

Status: First of two prototypes scheduled to commence its flight test programme April 1977.

Notes: The Fantrainer, by use of an integrated ducted-fan propulsion system, will simulate the characteristics of turbojet-powered aircraft but offers appreciably lower operating costs and is intended to cover all phases of the training spectrum up to such types as the Alpha Jet. Two prototypes of the AWI-2 version of the Fantrainer have been ordered by the Federal Germany Ministry of Defence and these have essentially similar cockpits to those of the Alpha Jet (see pages 66—67). The coupled Wankel engines may be replaced by a single turboshaft of 400 eshp upwards, this variant of the Fantrainer being the ATI-2, and alternative wings are offered: application of a 34 ft 5⅓ in (10,50 m) wing resulting in the AWI-4 and ATI-4, and use of a 25 ft 10¼ in (7,88 m) wing producing the ATI-2K1.

RFB FANTRAINER AWI-2

Dimensions: Span, 31 ft 5$\frac{9}{10}$ in (9,60 m); length, 26 ft 3$\frac{3}{4}$ in (8,02 m); height, 9 ft 6$\frac{1}{8}$ in (2,90 m); wing area, 149·6 sq ft (13,90 m²).

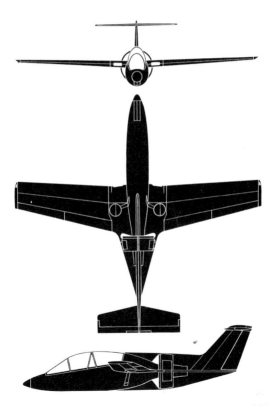

ROCKWELL (FUJI) COMMANDER 700

Countries of Origin: USA and Japan.

Type: Light cabin monoplane.

Power Plant: Two 325 hp Avco Lycoming TIO-540-R2AD six-cylinder horizontally-opposed engines.

Performance: Max. speed, 266 mph (428 km/h) at 20,000 ft (6 095 m); cruise (at 75% power), 252 mph (405 km/h) at 24,000 ft (7 315 m), (at 45% power), 177 mph (285 km/h) at 15,000 ft (4 570 m); initial climb, 1,460 ft/min (7,4 m/sec); service ceiling, 30,400 ft (9 265 m); range (at 75% power), 810 mls (1 303 km).

Weights: Empty equipped, 4,400 lb (1 995 kg); max. take-off, 6,600 lb (2 993 kg).

Accommodation: Pilot and co-pilot in individual seats and seats for four to six passengers in pressurised cabin.

Status: Product of a joint design effort by Rockwell (USA) and Fuji (Japan), the first of four prototypes having flown (in Japan) on November 13, 1975, and the second (in the USA) on February 25, 1976. Production deliveries scheduled to commence during the course of 1977, with Fuji manufacturing the basic structure and Rockwell assembling and completing those intended for the American market.

Notes: The Commander 700 (known in Japan as the Fuji FA-300) is a collaborative venture launched in 1974 after more than two years of market research, 60% of the funding being provided by the Japanese company which is responsible for assembly of all aircraft for sale in the Far East. Derivatives of the basic design with uprated engines and with turboprops are currently under development.

ROCKWELL (FUJI) COMMANDER 700

Dimensions: Span, 42 ft 5½ in (12,94 m); length, 39 ft 4½ in (12,00 m); height, 12 ft 9½ in (3,90 m); wing area, 200·2 sq ft (18,60 m²).

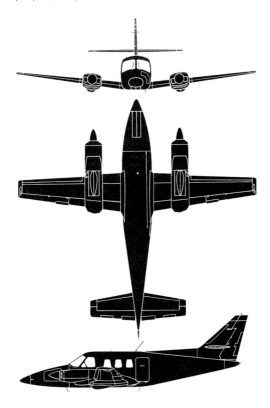

ROCKWELL INTERNATIONAL B-1

Country of Origin: USA.

Type: Strategic heavy bomber.

Power Plant: Four 17,000 lb (7 711 kg) dry and 30,000 lb (13 608 kg) reheat General Electric F101-GE-100 turbofans.

Performance: (Prototypes estimated) Max. speed, 1,450 mph (2 334 km/h) at 40,000 ft (12 190 m) or Mach 2·2, 900 mph (1 450 km/h) at 1,500 ft (460 m) or Mach 1·2, 648 mph (1 042 km/h) at sea level or Mach 0·85; max. range (internal fuel), 6,100 mls (9 820 km).

Weights: Max. take-off (design), 389,800 lb (176 822 kg).

Armament: Twenty-four Boeing AGM-69A SRAM (Short-Range Attack Missile) ASMs in three weapons bays, plus eight SRAMs on four underfuselage hardpoints. Max. permissible weapons load, 115,000 lb (52 160 kg).

Status: First of four prototypes flown December 23, 1974, with second and third flown on June 14 and April 1, 1976 respectively and fourth to fly in February 1979. Formal production programme initiated December 1976. USAF hopes to order 240 production B-1As.

Notes: The first three prototypes feature crew escape modules which, together with the planned variable-geometry engine intakes, are being deleted from later aircraft as economy measures. The fourth prototype will have separate ejection seats for the crew members, lighter nacelle intake structure, lighter wing carry-through structure and other changes to reduce structural weight by at least 10,000 lb (4 540 kg). The fixed intake geometry will result in a reduction of Mach 0·6 in the maximum attainable speed of the B-1A. The third prototype is equipped with the full offensive avionics system. The B-1A is intended as a replacement for the Boeing B-52 Stratofortress in the inventory of the USAF Strategic Aerospace Command in the 'eighties.

ROCKWELL INTERNATIONAL B-1

Dimensions: Span (max.), 136 ft 8½ in (41,66 m), (min.), 78 ft 2½ in (23,83 m); length (including probe), 150 ft 2½ in (45,80 m); height, 33 ft 7¼ in (10,24 m); wing area (approx.), 1,950 sq ft (181,2 m²).

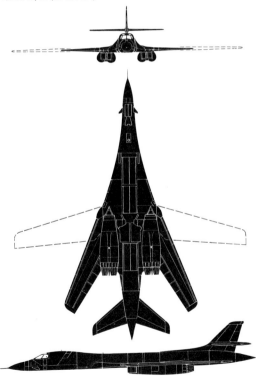

SAAB (JA) 37 VIGGEN

Country of Origin: Sweden.

Type: Single-seat all-weather intercepter fighter with secondary strike capability.

Power Plant: One 16,203 lb (7 350 kg) dry and 28,108 lb (12 750 kg) reheat Volvo Flygmotor RM 8B.

Performance: (Estimated) Max. speed (with two RB 24 Sidewinder AAMs), 1,320 mph (2 125 km/h) above 36,090 ft (11 000 m) or Mach 2·0, 910 mph (1 465 km/h) at 1,000 ft (305 m) or Mach 1·2; operational radius (M = 2·0 intercept with two AAMs), 250 mls (400 km), (lo-lo-lo ground attack with six Mk. 82 bombs), 300 mls (480 km); time (from brakes off) to 32,810 ft (10 000 m), 1·4 min.

Weights: (Estimated) Empty, 26,895 lb (12 200 kg); loaded (two AAMs), 37,040 lb (16 800 kg); max. take-off, 49,600 lb (22 500 kg).

Armament: One semi-externally mounted 30-mm Oerlikon KCA cannon with 150 rounds and up to 13,227 lb (6 000 kg) of ordnance on seven (three fuselage and four wing) external stores stations, including Saab 372 infra-red and RB 71 (HS SkyFlash) radar homing AAMs.

Status: First of four JA 37 prototypes (modified from AJ 37 airframes) flown June 1974, with fifth prototype built from outset to JA 37 standards flown December 15, 1975. Initial production contract for 30 JA 37 Viggens placed late 1974 against anticipated procurement of 150–200 aircraft with first due to fly late 1977.

Notes: The JA 37 is a development of the AJ 37 (see 1973 edition) which is optimised for the attack role, the SF 37 (see 1974 edition) and SH 37 being respectively tactical reconnaissance and sea surveillance derivatives of the latter. The JA 37 has uprated turbofan, cannon armament and X-Band Pulse Doppler radar.

SAAB (JA) 37 VIGGEN

Dimensions: Span, 34 ft 9¼ in (10,60 m); length (excluding probe), 50 ft 8¼ in (15,45 m); height, 19 ft 4¼ in (5,90 m); wing area (including foreplanes), 561·88 sq ft (52,20 m²).

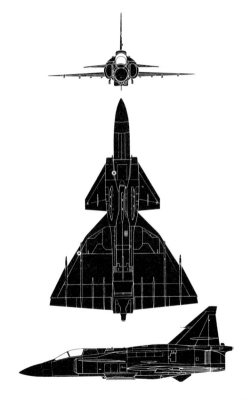

SCOTTISH AVIATION BULLFINCH

Country of Origin: United Kingdom.

Type: Light cabin monoplane.

Power Plant: One 200 bhp Avco Lycoming AEIO-360-A1B6 four-cylinder horizontally-opposed engine.

Performance: (At 2,304 lb/1 045 kg) Max. speed, 173 mph (278 km/h) at sea level; cruise (75% power), 162 mph (261 km/h) at 4,000 ft (1 220 m); initial climb, 1,160 ft/min (5,88 m/sec); service ceiling, 18,500 ft (5 640 m); max. range (55% power), 622 mls (1 000 km).

Weights: Typical operational empty, 1,810 lb (820 kg); max. aerobatic, 2,304 lb (1 045 kg); max. take-off, 2,601 lb (1 180 kg).

Accommodation: Four individual seats with dual controls.

Status: Bullfinch prototype first flown on August 20, 1976, with production deliveries of this and equivalent military Bulldog 200 offered for early 1978.

Notes: The civil Bullfinch and the military Bulldog 200 are progressive developments of the fixed-gear Bulldog 120 (see 1974 edition) which continues in production. Compared with the Bulldog 120, the Bullfinch and Bulldog 200 are 20 in (51 cm) longer, have a 9·3-in (23,6-cm) increase in wing span, a relocated tailplane and four-seat capacity. The Bullfinch has two-seat aerobatic capability and the Bulldog 200 complements but does not supplant the fixed-gear Bulldog 120. The Bulldog 200 is suitable for basic and aerobatic training, liaison, light strike, forward air control and weapon training, and features four wing hardpoints with a combined capacity of 640 lb (290 kg) of ordnance. Both the Bullfinch and Bulldog 200 are fully aerobatic, being stressed to plus 6g and minus 3g.

SCOTTISH AVIATION BULLFINCH

Dimensions: Span, 33 ft 9$\frac{3}{10}$ in (10,29 m); length, 24 ft 11 in (7,59 m); height, 8 ft 4 in (2,54 m).

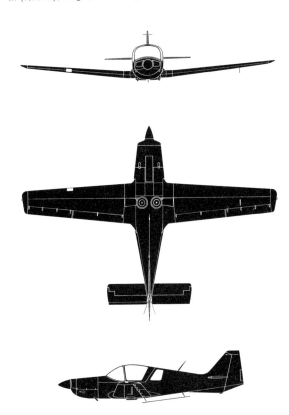

SEPECAT JAGUAR G.R. MK. 1

Countries of Origin: France and United Kingdom.
Type: Single-seat tactical strike fighter.
Power Plant: Two 4,620 lb (2 100 kg) dry and 7,140 lb (3 240 kg) reheat Rolls-Royce Turboméca RT.172 Adour 102 turbofans.
Performance: (At typical weight) Max. speed, 820 mph (1 320 km/h) or Mach 1·1 at 1,000 ft (305 m), 1,057 mph (1 700 km/h) or Mach 1·6 at 32,810 ft (10 000 m); cruise with max. ordnance, 430 mph (690 km/h) or Mach 0·65 at 39,370 ft (12 000 m); range with external fuel for lo-lo-lo mission profile, 450 mls (724 km), for hi-lo-hi mission profile, 710 mls (1 142 km); ferry range, 2,270 mls (3 650 km).
Weights: Normal take-off, 23,000 lb (10 430 kg); max. take-off, 32,600 lb (14 790 kg).
Armament: Two 30-mm Aden cannon and up to 10,000 lb (4 536 kg) ordnance on five external hardpoints.
Status: First of eight prototypes flown September 8, 1968. First production Jaguar E for France flown November 2, 1971, with first Jaguar A following April 20, 1972. First production Jaguar S for UK flown October 11, 1972. By the beginning of 1977, France had ordered 180 Jaguars and the UK had ordered 202.
Notes: Both France and UK have a requirement for approximately 200 Jaguars, French versions being the single-seat A (*Appui Tactique*) and two-seat E (*École de Combat*), and British versions being the single-seat S (G.R. Mk. 1) and the two-seat B (T Mk. 2). The export Jaguar International with uprated Adour 804 engines (illustrated above with overwing-mounted Magic AAMs) has been ordered by Oman (12) and Ecuador (12) with deliveries to the former scheduled for early 1977.

SEPECAT JAGUAR G.R. MK. 1

Dimensions: Span, 28 ft 6 in (8,69 m); length, 50 ft 11 in (15,52 m); height, 16 ft 0½ in (4,89 m); wing area, 260·3 sq ft (24,18 m²).

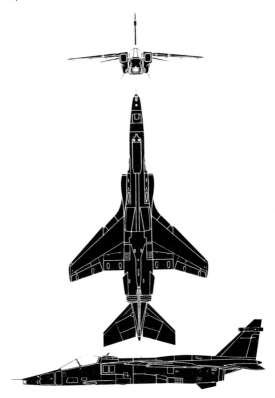

SHINMEIWA US-1 OHTORI

Country of Origin: Japan.

Type: Amphibious search and rescue flying boat.

Power Plant: Four 3,060 ehp Ishikawajima-Harima-built General Electric T64-IHI-10 turboprops.

Performance: Max. speed, 299 mph (481 km/h) at 9,840 ft (3 000 m); high-speed cruise, 265 mph (426 km/h) at 9,840 ft (3 000 m); long-range cruise (two engines), 202 mph (325 km/h) at 8,200 ft (2 500 m); loiter speed, 161 mph (259 km/h) at 1,000 ft (305 m); search endurance, 6 hrs at 690-mile (1 110 km) range; max. search and rescue range, 3,145 mls (5 060 km); initial climb, 2,360 ft/min (12,0 m/sec); service ceiling, 28,000 ft (8 535 m).

Weights: Empty equipped, 56,218 lb (25 500 kg); max. take-off, 99,208 lb (45 000 kg).

Accommodation: Crew of eight comprising pilot, co-pilot, flight engineer, radar operator, navigator, radio operator, observer and rescue man. Up to five medical attendants and 36 stretcher casualties.

Status: First of three US-1s ordered by the Japanese Maritime Self-Defence Force flown October 16, 1974, and delivered March 1975, with second and third aircraft following in June and December respectively. Development continuing.

Notes: The US-1 (alias SS-2A) is an amphibious rescue derivative of the SS-2 maritime patrol flying boat (see 1974 edition). Featuring a retractable undercarriage, the main twinwheel members of which retract into bulged housings, the US-1 has a 1,400 ehp General Electric T58-10 turboshaft driving a boundary-layer control compressor for the flaps, elevators and rudder. The US-1 has been named Ohtori (a mythical bird) by the JMSDF.

SHINMEIWA US-1 OHTORI

Dimensions: Span, 107 ft 6½ in (32,78 m); length, 109 ft 11 in (33,50 m); height, 32 ft 3 in (9,83 m); wing area, 1,453·13 sq ft (135,00 m²).

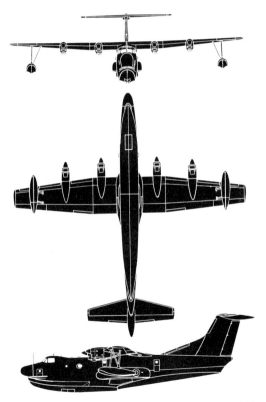

SHORTS SD3-30

Country of Origin: United Kingdom.

Type: Third-level airliner and utility transport.

Power Plant: Two 1,120 shp Pratt & Whitney (Canada) PT6A-45 turboprops.

Performance: (At 20,000 lb/9 072 kg) Max. cruise, 227 mph (365 km/h) at 10,000 ft (3 050 m); econ. cruise, 184 mph (297 km/h) at 10,000 ft (3 050 m); range (no reserves) with 30 passengers and baggage (5,940 lb/2 694 kg), 500 mls (800 km); ferry range, 1,150 mls (1 850 km); max. climb, 1,210 ft/min (6,14 m/sec).

Weights: Empty equipped (for 30 passengers), 14,200 lb (6 441 kg); max. take-off, 22,000 lb (9 979 kg).

Accommodation: Standard flight crew of two and normal accommodation for 30 passengers in 10 rows three abreast and 1,000 lb (455 kg) of baggage.

Status: Engineering prototype flown August 22, 1974, with production prototype following on July 8, 1975. First production aircraft flown on December 15, 1975, with third being first customer delivery example (to Command Airways on June 28, 1976). Orders by beginning of 1977 included three for Command Airways, three for Time Air and one (with a second on option) for the Federal German DLT third-level operator.

Notes: Intended primarily for commuter and regional air service operators, the SD3-30 is also being offered for the military tactical transport role as the SD3-M, other missions including coastal patrol and reconnaissance, casualty evacuation, search and rescue, and aerial survey. The SD3-M will accommodate 31 fully-equipped paratroops and will feature a large rear-loading door.

SHORTS SD3-30

Dimensions: Span, 74 ft 8 in (22,76 m); length, 58 ft 0½ in (17,69 m); height, 16 ft 3 in (4,95 m); wing area, 453 sq ft (42,10 m²).

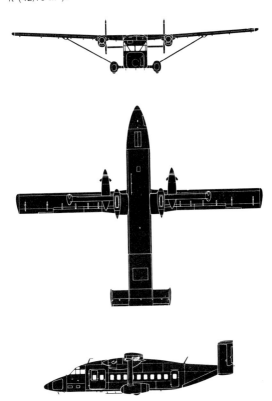

SIAI-MARCHETTI SM.1019E

Country of Origin: Italy.

Type: Battlefield surveillance and forward air control aircraft.

Power Plant: One 400 shp Allison 250-B17 turboprop.

Performance: Max. speed, 181 mph (287 km/h) at sea level; max. cruise (75% power), 146 mph (235 km/h) at sea level, 149 mph (239 km/h) at 9,850 ft (3 000 m); max. range, 702 mls (1 130 km) at sea level, 832 mls (1 340 km) at 10,000 ft (3 050 m); initial climb, 1,319 ft/min (6,7 m/sec); service ceiling, 21,325 ft (6 500 m).

Weights: Empty equipped, 1,521 lb (690 kg); max. take-off, 3,196 lb (1 450 kg).

Armament: Two stores stations under wings capable of carrying Minigun pods, rockets, etc, up to a maximum external load of 500 lb (227 kg).

Status: First prototype flown May 24, 1969, with second prototype (SM.1019A) following on February 18, 1971. Deliveries of initial production batch of 40 (SM.1019E) begun mid-1975 against total Italian Army requirement for 80 aircraft programmed for completion by mid-1977.

Notes: The SM.1019 is based upon the Cessna O-1 Bird Dog but possesses an extensively modified airframe to meet latest operational requirements, redesigned tail surfaces and a turboprop in place of the O-1's piston engine. Whereas the second prototype, the SM.1019A (see 1975 edition), had a 317 shp Allison 250-B15G turboprop, the more powerful 250-B17 has been standardised for the production SM.1019E. The pilot and co-pilot or observer/systems operator are seated in tandem and dual controls are optional.

SIAI-MARCHETTI SM.1019E

Dimensions: Span, 36 ft 0 in (10,97 m); length, 27 ft 10⅔ in (8,52 m); height, 9 ft 4½ in (2,86 m); wing area, 173·94 sq ft (16,16 m²).

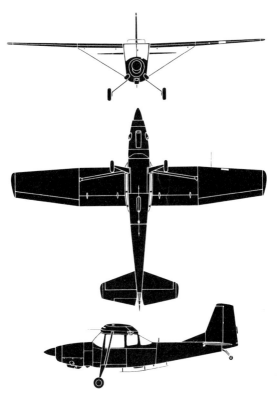

SPORTAVIA RF6-180 SPORTSMAN

Country of Origin: Federal Germany.

Type: Light cabin monoplane.

Power Plant: One 180 hp Avco Lycoming O-360-A1F6D four-cylinder horizontally-opposed engine.

Performance: Cruise at 8,500 ft/2 590 m (75% power), 168 mph (270 km/h), (65% power), 154 mph (248 km/h), (55% power), 142 mph (228 km/h); max. range (no reserves), 938 mls (1 510 km); initial climb, 1,060 ft/min (5,40 m/sec).

Weights: Empty, 1,312 lb (595 kg); max. take-off, 2,425 lb (1 100 kg).

Accommodation: Four individual seats in side-by-side pairs enclosed by two-piece canopy. Full dual controls.

Status: Prototype flown as RF6-125 (with 2+2 accommodation) flown on March 1, 1973. Subsequently re-engined and extensively modified to provide full four-seat accommodation and flown for first time in revised form (as RF6-180) on April 28, 1976. First production deliveries expected for March 1977.

Notes: The RF6-180 is an uprated and improved derivative of the RF6 designed for Sportavia-Pützer, a subsidiary of VFW-Fokker, by René Fournier (variants of the basic design being built by Avions Fournier in France). Since the initial prototype was flown, the RF6 has been extensively developed, a larger cabin being introduced (within the same overall dimensions) with a redesigned canopy, together with numerous other changes.

SPORTAVIA RF6-180 SPORTSMAN

Dimensions: Span, 34 ft 5⅓ in (10,50 m); length, 23 ft 5½ in (7,15 m); height, 8 ft 4 in (2,56 m); wing area, 156·08 sq ft (14,50 m²).

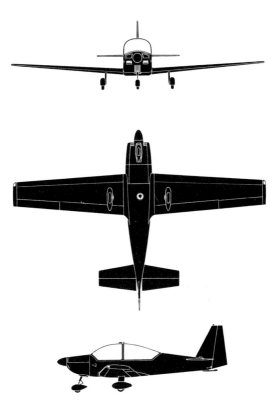

SUKHOI SU-17 (FITTER-C)

Country of Origin: USSR.

Type: Single-seat tactical strike fighter.

Power Plant: One 17,195 lb (7 800 kg) dry and 24,700 lb (11 200 kg) reheat Lyulka AL-21F-3 turbojet.

Performance: Max. speed (clean), 808 mph (1 300 km/h) or Mach 1·06 at sea level, 1,430 mph (2 300 km/h) at 39,370 ft (12 000 m) or Mach 2·17; combat radius (lo-lo-lo mission profile), 260 mls (420 km), (hi-lo-hi mission profile), 373 mls (600 km); range (with 2,205-lb/1 000-kg weapon load and auxiliary fuel), 1,415 mls (2 280 km); service ceiling, 57,415 ft (17 500 m).

Weights: Max. take-off, 39,022 lb (17 700 kg).

Armament: Two 30-mm NR-30 cannon with 70 rpg and (for short-range missions) a max. external ordnance load of 7,716 lb (3 500 kg). Typical external stores include UV-16-57 or UV-32-57 rocket pods containing 16 and 32 55-mm S-5 rockets respectively, 240-mm S-24 rockets, two AS-7 Kerry ASMs, or 550-lb (250-kg) or 1,100-lb (500-kg) bombs.

Status: The Su-17 entered service with the Soviet Air Forces in 1972, and is currently being exported to Warsaw Pact countries, having entered service with the Polish Air Force during the course of 1974.

Notes: The Su-17 is a variable-geometry derivative of the Su-7 Fitter-A (see 1973 edition). Intended primarily for the close air support, battlefield interdiction and counterair roles, but with secondary combat zone air superiority capability, the Su-17 has been offered for export under the designations Su-20 and Su-22 (the latter being purchased by Peru), these differing in equipment standards.

SUKHOI SU-17 (FITTER-C)

Estimated Dimensions: Span (max.), 45 ft 0 in (13,70 m), (min.), 32 ft 6 in (9,90 m) ; length (including probe), 57 ft 0 in (17,37 m) ; height, 15 ft 5 in (4,70 m).

SUKHOI SU-19 (FENCER-A)

Country of Origin: USSR.

Type: Two-seat ground attack fighter.

Power Plant: Two (estimated) 13,230 lb (6 000 kg) dry and 19,840 lb (9 000 kg) reheat turbojets.

Performance: (Estimated) Max. speed, 760–840 mph (1 225–1 350 km/h) at sea level or Mach 1·0–1·1, 1,385–1,520 mph (2 230–2 445 km/h) at 36,090 ft (11 000 m) or Mach 2·1–2·3; radius of action (lo-lo-lo), 250 mls (400 km), (hi-lo-hi), 750 mls (1 200 km); max. endurance, 3–4 hrs.

Weights: (Estimated) Empty equipped, 33,000 lb (14 970 kg); max. take-off, 68,000 lb (30 845 kg).

Armament: One six-barrel 23-mm rotary cannon in the underside of the fuselage and up to 10,000–11,000 lb (4 500–5 000 kg) of ordnance on six external stations (two under the fuselage and four under the fixed wing glove), a typical ordnance load comprising two 1,100-lb (500-kg) bombs, two surface-to-air missiles and two pods each containing 16 or 32 57-mm unguided rockets.

Status: Prototypes of the Su-19 are believed to have flown in 1970, and this type was first reported to be in service with the Soviet Air Forces during the course of 1974. Western intelligence agencies indicated that some two hundred will have attained service by mid-1977.

Notes: The Su-19 (the accompanying illustrations of which should be considered as provisional) is the first Soviet fighter optimised for the ground attack role to have achieved service status. Wing leading-edge sweep varies from approximately 23 deg fully spread to 70 deg fully swept, and the wings reportedly incorporate both leading- and trailing-edge lift devices and lift dumpers acting as spoilers in conjunction with differential tailplane movement for roll control.

SUKHOI SU-19 (FENCER-A)

Dimensions: (Estimated): Span (max.), 56 ft (17,00 m), (min.), 31 ft (9,45 m); length, 70 ft (21,35 m).

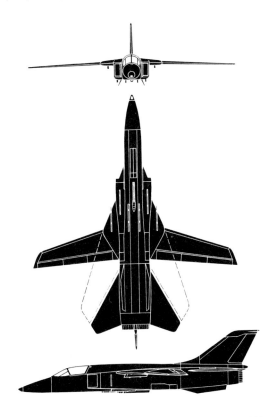

TUPOLEV (BACKFIRE-B)

Country of Origin: USSR.

Type: Strategic bomber.

Power Plant: Two (estimated) 33,070 lb (15 000 kg) dry and 46,300 lb (21 000 kg) reheat Kuznetsov turbofans.

Performance: (Estimated) Max. speed, 685 mph (1 100 km/h) or Mach 0·9 at sea level, 1,320 mph (2 125 km/h) at 39,370 ft (12 000 m) or Mach 2·0; combat radius (lo-lo-lo), 1,240 mls (2 000 km), (hi-lo-hi), 2,485 mls (4 000 km), (hi-hi-hi), 3,730 mls (6 000 km); service ceiling, 59,000 ft (18 000 m).

Weights: (Estimated) Empty equipped, 121,255 lb (55 000 kg); max. take-off, 297,625 lb (135 000 kg).

Armament: (Defensive) Remotely-controlled 23-mm cannon in tail barbette. Internal bomb load of up to 16,000 lb (7 250 kg) or two externally-mounted 9,920-lb (4 500-kg) AS-6 stand-off missiles with (approx·) 460-mile (740-km) range and inertial guidance.

Status: First reported in prototype form in 1969, the Backfire began to enter service with both the Soviet long-range aviation component and the Naval Air Force during the course of 1974, production reportedly running at 15 per year at the beginning of 1977 when 60–70 were believed in service.

Notes: The Backfire-B (the design bureau designation of which was unknown at the time of closing for press) has been the subject of considerable contention in relation to the Strategic Arms Limitation Talks (SALT), the Soviet Union alleging that it does not possess intercontinental range.

192

TUPOLEV (BACKFIRE-B)

Dimensions: (Estimated) Span (max.), 115 ft 0 in (35,00 m), (min.), 92 ft 0 in (28,00 m); length, 138 ft 0 in (42,00 m); height, 29 ft 6 in (9,00 m).

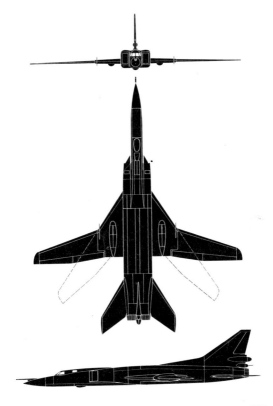

TUPOLEV TU-22 (BLINDER)

Country of Origin: USSR.

Type: Medium bomber and strike-reconnaissance aircraft.

Power Plant: Two (approx.) 15,000 lb (6 800 kg) dry and 27,000 lb (12 250 kg) reheat turbojets.

Performance: (Estimated) Max. speed (clean), 860 mph (1 385 km/h) at 36,090 ft (11 000 m) or Mach 1·3, 685 mph (1 100 km/h) at 1,000 ft (300 m) or Mach 0·9; tactical radius (hi-lo-hi), 1,370 mls (2 200 km) at 530 mph (850 km/h) or Mach 0·8.

Weights: Max. take-off (estimated), 185,000 lb (84 000 kg).

Armament: Internally-housed free-falling weapons or (Blinder-B) semi-recessed AS-4 Kitchen stand-off missile. Remotely-controlled 23-mm cannon in tail barbette.

Status: Believed to have attained operational status with the Soviet Air Forces in 1965. Limited production believed continuing into 1977.

Notes: Variants include (Blinder-A) standard bomber and strike aircraft and (Blinder-B) its missile-carrying version, (Blinder-C) a maritime reconnaissance model, (Blinder-D) an operational trainer, and a long-range heavy interceptor for periphery defence.

TUPOLEV TU-22 (BLINDER)

Dimensions: (Estimated) Span, 91 ft 0 in (27,74 m); length, 133 ft 0 in (40,50 m); height, 17 ft 0 in (5,18 m); wing area, 2,030 sq ft (188,59 m²).

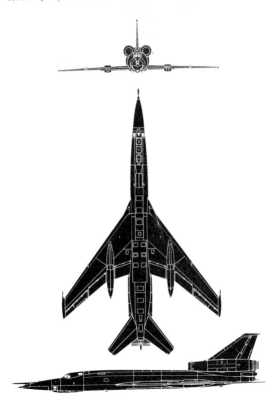

TUPOLEV TU-126 (MOSS)

Country of Origin: USSR.

Type: Airborne warning and control system aircraft.

Power Plant: Four 14,795 ehp Kuznetsov NK-12MV turbo-props.

Performance: (Estimated) Max. speed, 510 mph (820 km/h); max. continuous cruise, 460 mph (740 km/h) at 25,000 ft (7 620 m); operational cruise, 410 mph (660 km/h) at 21,325 ft (6 500 m); mission endurance (unrefuelled), 9 hrs at 620-mile (1 000-km) radius, 6 hrs at 1,240-mile (2 000-km) radius; service ceiling, 36,090 ft (11 000 m).

Weights: (Estimated) Normal max. take-off, 360,000 lb (163,290 kg).

Status: The Tu-126 AWACS aircraft is believed to have flown in prototype form in 1962–63 and first appeared in service with the Soviet Air Forces in the late 'sixties. Some 20–30 aircraft of this type are believed to be in service.

Notes: Essentially an adaptation of the Tu-114 commercial transport and retaining basically similar wings, tail surfaces power plant and undercarriage to those of the earlier aircraft, the Tu-126 is primarily intended to locate low-flying intruders and to vector interceptors towards them. The dominating feature of the aircraft is its pylon-mounted saucer-shaped early-warning scanner. The Tu-126 reportedly operates most effectively over water, possessing only limited overland "look-down" capability.

TUPOLEV TU-126 (MOSS)

Dimensions: Span, 168 ft 0 in (51,20 m); approx. length, 188 ft 0 in (57,30 m); height, 51 ft 0 in (15,50 m); wing area, 3,349 sq ft (311,1 m²).

TUPOLEV TU-134A (CRUSTY)

Country of Origin: USSR.

Type: Short- to medium-range commercial transport.

Power Plant: Two 14,990 lb (6 800 kg) Soloviev D-30-2 Turbofans.

Performance: Max. cruise, 528 mph (850 km/h) at 32,810 ft (10 000 m); long-range cruise, 466 mph (750 km/h) at 32,810 ft (10 000 m); max. range at long-range cruise with 1 hr reserves and 18,108-lb (8 215-kg) payload, 1,243 mls (2 000 km), with 8,818-lb (4 000-kg) payload, 2,175 mls (3 500 km).

Weights: Operational empty, 63,934 lb (29 000 kg); max. take-off, 103,617 lb (47 000 kg).

Accommodation: Basic flight crew of three and maximum of 80 passengers in four-abreast all-tourist class configuration.

Status: Prototype Tu-134A flown in 1968 and first production deliveries (to *Aeroflot*) mid-1970. Series production continuing at Kharkov at the beginning of 1977.

Notes: The Tu-134A differs from the original Tu-134, which entered *Aeroflot* service in 1966, in having an additional 6 ft 10⅔ in (2,10 m) section inserted in the fuselage immediately forward of the wing to permit two additional rows of passenger seats, and introduces engine thrust reversers. Maximum take-off weight has been increased by 5,512 lb (2 500 kg), maximum payload being raised by 1,025 lb (465 kg), an APU is provided, and radio and navigational equipment have been revised. Route proving trials with the Tu-134A were completed by *Aeroflot* late in 1970, and this airliner was introduced on international routes early in 1971. The shorter-fuselage Tu-134 serves with Aeroflot, CSA, Interflug, LOT, Malev, Balkan-Bulgarian and Aviogenex.

TUPOLEV TU-134A (CRUSTY)

Dimensions: Span, 95 ft 2 in (29,00 m); length, 111 ft 0½ in (36,40 m); height, 29 ft 7 in (9,02 m); wing area, 1,370·3 sq ft (127,3 m²).

TUPOLEV TU-144 (CHARGER)

Country of Origin: USSR.

Type: Long-range supersonic commercial transport.

Power Plant: Four 33,100 lb (15 000 kg) dry and 44,000 lb (20 000 kg) reheat Kuznetsov NK-144 turbofans.

Performance: Max. cruise, 1,550 mph (2 500 km/h) or Mach 2·3 at altitudes up to 59,000 ft (18 000 m); subsonic cruise, 614 mph (988 km/h) or Mach 0·93 at 37,730 ft (11 500 m); range (with full payload), 4,000 mls (6 440 km); cruising altitude, 52,500 ft (16 460 m) to 59,000 ft (18 000 m).

Weights: Typical operational empty, 187,395 lb (85 000 kg); max. take-off, 396,830 lb (180 000 kg).

Accommodation: Basic flight crew of three and maximum of up to 140 passengers in single-class arrangement with three-plus-two and two-plus-two seating.

Status: First pre-production aircraft (representative of the production configuration) flown September 1971, and six aircraft of production standard had reportedly flown by mid-1975 when a further 12 were alleged to be under construction against an anticipated Aeroflot requirement for approximately 30 aircraft. Scheduled service (freight only) between Moscow and Alma Ata began December 26, 1975, and was suspended in November 1976, and initial passenger services had not begun by the beginning of 1977.

Notes: The production-standard Tu-144 described and illustrated on these pages shares little more than a generally similar configuration with the prototype to which this designation was first applied and which flew for the first time on December 31, 1968. The current model has been lengthened by 20 ft 8 in (6,30 m) and the compound delta wing is of 3 ft 9 in (1,15 m) greater span than the ogee wing of the original aircraft.

TUPOLEV TU-144 (CHARGER)

Dimensions: Span, 94 ft 6 in (28,80 m); length, 215 ft 6½ in (65,70 m); height, 42 ft 3 in (12,85 m); wing area, 4,720 sq ft (438 m²).

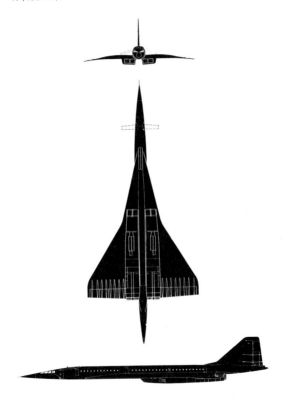

TUPOLEV TU-154A (CARELESS)

Country of Origin: USSR.

Type: Medium- to long-haul commercial transport.

Power Plant: Three 23,150 lb (10 500 kg) Kuznetsov NK-8-2U turbofans.

Performance: Max. cruise, 590 mph (950 km/h) at 31,170 ft (9 500 m); econ. cruise, 559 mph (900 km/h); range (with normal reserves and 39,683-lb/18 000-kg payload), 1,864 mls (3 000 km), (with 35,274-lb/16 000-kg payload), 2,050 mls (3 300 km), (with 27,557-lb/12 500-kg payload), 2,485 mls (4 000 km).

Weights: Max. take-off, 207,235 lb (94 00 kg).

Accommodation: Flight crew of three–four and basic arrangements for 152 or 168 passengers in six-abreast seating.

Status: Developed from the original Tu-154 (which flew as a prototype on October 4, 1968), the Tu-154A first flew late 1973 and entered Aeroflot service during April 1974.

Notes: The principal difference between the Tu-154A and the original Tu-154 (see 1975 edition) is the use of uprated engines which permit an 8,818-lb (4 000-kg) increase in max. take-off weight. An extra fuel tank is installed in the centre section. The Tu-154A can operate from airfields with category B surfaces, including packed earth and gravel. Operators of the earlier Tu-154 (which the Tu-154A has replaced in production) include Balkan-Bulgarian and Malev of Hungary. The latest standard production version is reportedly the Tu-154V with revised navigational equipment and a modified arrangement of emergency exits. The Tu-154V has superseded the Tu-154A in production, and versions with greater weight and range are known to be under study.

TUPOLEV TU-154A (CARELESS)

Dimensions: Span, 123 ft 2½ in (37,55 m); length, 157 ft 1¾ in (47,90 m); height, 37 ft 4¾ in (11,40 m); wing area, 2,168·92 sq ft (201,45 m²).

VALMET LEKO-70

Country of Origin: Finland.

Type: Side-by-side two-seat primary trainer.

Power Plant: One 200 hp Avco Lycoming IO-360-A1B6 four-cylinder horizontally-opposed engine.

Performance: Max. speed, 149 mph (240 km/h) at sea level; max. initial climb, 1,180 ft/min (6,0 m/sec). No further details available for publication.

Weights: Empty equipped (prototype), 1,587 lb (720 kg), (production), 1,521 lb (690 kg); max. take-off, 2,535 lb (1 150 kg).

Status: Prototype flown July 1, 1975, with production expected to commence during the course of 1977 against a Finnish Air Force requirement for 30 aircraft, with deliveries commencing in 1979.

Notes: Intended to succeed the Saab 91D Safir as the standard Finnish Air Force primary trainer and the first new military aircraft of Finnish design to fly since the Tuuli III primary trainer prototype of 1957, the Leko-70 is also envisaged as a touring aircraft with provision for a third seat at the rear of the cabin which may be removed to provide space for additional baggage. As a two-seater, the Leko-70 is fully aerobatic. Designed by the aeronautical research and development group at the Tampere works of the state-owned Valmet Oy, the Leko-70 was ordered as a prototype by the Finnish Air Force on March 23, 1973, and the data quoted above are based on design estimates and had still to be confirmed by the flight test programme at the time of closing for press.

VALMET LEKO-70

Dimensions: Span, 30 ft $6\frac{1}{4}$ in (9,30 m); length, 23 ft $11\frac{1}{2}$ in (7,30 m); wing area, 150·69 sq ft (14,00 m²).

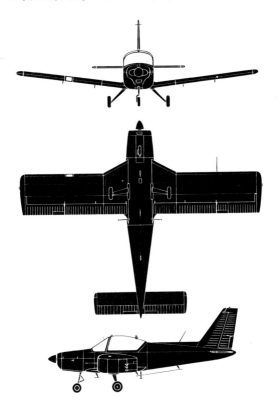

VFW-FOKKER VFW 614

Country of Origin: Federal Germany.
Type: Short-haul commercial transport.
Power Plant: Two 7,280 lb (3 302 kg) Rolls-Royce/
SNECMA M45H Mk. 501 turbofans.
Performance: Max. speed, 457 mph (735 km/h) at 21,000
ft (6 400 m); max. cruise, 449 mph (722 km/h) at 25,000 ft
(7 620 m); long-range cruise, 367 mph (591 km/h) at 25,000
ft (7 620 m); max. fuel range (with reserves), 1,249 mls (2 010
km); range (40 passengers and reserves), 748 mls (1 205 km);
max. climb, 3,100 ft/min (15,75 m/sec); service ceiling, 25,000
ft (7 620 m).
Weights: Operational empty, 26,850 lb (12 180 kg); max.
take-off, 44,000 lb (19 950 kg).
Accommodation: Basic flight crew of two and standard layout for 40 passengers in rows of four. Alternative arrangement
for 44 passengers.
Status: First of three flying prototypes commenced test programme on July 14, 1971, with first production aircraft flying
on April 28, 1975. This was delivered to Cimber Air in August
1975. Production of 30 authorised with orders for 16 (two for
Cimber Air, eight for Touraine Air Transport, three for Air Alsace
and three for the Federal German government) recorded by
beginning of 1977.
Notes: VFW 614 is a collaborative production programme
under the leadership of VFW-Fokker, participants including the
Dutch Fokker-VFW and Belgian SABCA and Fairey concerns.
Planning for a stretched version with accommodation for up
to 50 passengers was proceeding at the beginning of 1977.

VFW-FOKKER VFW 614

Dimensions: Span, 70 ft 6½ in (21,50 m); length, 67 ft 7 in (20,60 m); height, 25 ft 8 in (7,84 m); wing area, 688·89 sq ft (64,00 m²).

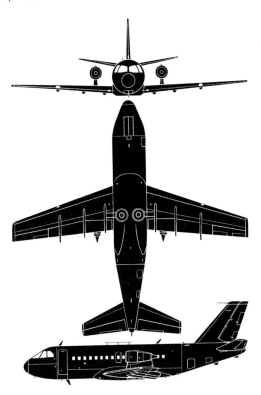

WSK-MIELEC M-15

Country of Origin: Poland.

Type: Three-seat agricultural biplane.

Power Plant: One 3,307 lb (1 500 kg) Ivchenko AI-25 turbo-fan.

Performance: Max. cruise, 124 mph (200 km/h); normal operating speed, 92–99 mph (145–160 km/h); max. range, 372 mls (600 km) at 9,850 ft (3 000 m); initial climb, 880 ft/min (4,48 m/sec).

Weights: Empty equipped, 6,393 lb (2 900 kg); max. take-off, 12,456 lb (5 650 kg).

Status: Aerodynamic prototype (LLP-M15) flown May 20, 1973, followed by first representative prototype on January 9, 1974. First batch of five of initial pre-production batch of 20 aircraft delivered to USSR for trials on April 26, 1975. Soviet Government reportedly has a requirement for up to 3,000 air-craft in this category.

Notes: The world's first turbine-powered biplane, the M-15 has been evolved by a joint Polish–Soviet team. The twin chemical containers between the wings have a combined capacity of 638 Imp gal (2 900 l) of liquid or 4,850 lb (2 200 kg) of dry chemicals. The M-15 is intended to supplant the Antonov An-2 biplane in the agricultural role.

WSK-MIELEC M-15

Dimensions: Span, 72 ft 0½ in (21,96 m); length, 41 ft 8¾ in (12,72 m); height, 17 ft 6½ in (5,34 m); wing area, 723·33 sq ft (67,20 m²).

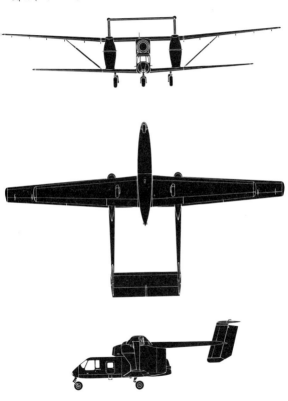

YAKOVLEV YAK-40 (CODLING)

Country of Origin: USSR.

Type: Short-range commercial feederliner.

Power Plant: Three 3,307 lb (1 500 kg) Ivchenko AI-25 or 3,858 lb (1 750 kg) AI-25T turbofans.

Performance: Max. speed, 373 mph (600 km/h) at sea level, 466 mph (750 km/h) at 17,000 ft (5 180 m); max. cruise, 342 mph (550 km/h) at 19,685 ft (6 000 m); econ. cruise, 310 mph (500 km/h) at 32,810 ft (10 000 m); range with 5,070-lb (2 300-kg) payload at econ. cruise, 620 mls (1 000 km), with 3,140-lb (1 425-kg) payload and max. fuel, 920 mls (1 480 km); initial climb, 2,000 ft/min (10,16 m/sec); service ceiling at max. loaded weight, 38,715 ft (11 800 m).

Weights: Empty equipped, 19,865–21,715 lb (9 010–9 850 kg); normal take-off, 27,250–34,170 lb (12 360–15 500 kg); max. take-off, 36,375 lb (16 500 kg).

Accommodation: Flight crew of two, and alternative arrangements for 27 or 34 passengers in three-abreast rows. High-density arrangement for 40 passengers in four-abreast rows, and executive configuration for 8–10 passengers.

Status: First of five prototypes flown October 21, 1966, and first production deliveries (to Aeroflot) mid-1968, the 500th example being completed on February 15, 1974.

Notes: Late 1976, a version of the Yak-40 referred to as the X-Avia was being promoted in the USA by ICX Aviation of Washington. The X-Avia is essentially the mating of the Soviet Yak-40 airframe with the US Garrett AiResearch TFE 731-2 turbofans. First deliveries are offered for late 1978 or early 1979.

YAKOVLEV YAK-40 (CODLING)

Dimensions: Span, 82 ft 0¼ in (25,00 m); length, 66 ft 9½ in (20,36 m); height, 21 ft 4 in (6,50 m); wing area, 753·473 sq ft (70 m²).

YAKOVLEV YAK-42

Country of Origin: USSR.

Type: Short- to medium-haul commercial transport.

Power Plant: Three 14,200 lb (6 440 kg) Lotarev D-36 turbofans.

Performance: Max. cruise, 528 mph (850 km/h) at 32,810 ft (10 000 m); econ. cruise, 503 mph (810 km/h) at 26,250 ft (8 000 m); range with max. payload (30,850 lb/14 000 kg), 1,118 mls (1 800 km), with max. fuel, 1,740 mls (2,800 km); time to cruise altitude (26,250 ft/8 000 m), 11 min.

Weights: Max. take-off, 114,640 lb (52 000 kg).

Accommodation: Flight crew of two and standard single-class six-abreast seating for 102 passengers. Alternative arrangement for 120 passengers.

Status: First of two prototypes flown on March 7, 1975. Production deliveries are expected to begin by late 1978 or early 1979.

Notes: Intended for operation over stages ranging from 248 mls (400 km) to 1,678 mls (2 700 km) and utilising restricted airfields with poor surfaces and limited facilities in the remoter areas of the Soviet Union in temperatures ranging from −50°C to +50°C, the Yak-42 is independent of airport ground equipment and a heavy-duty undercarriage caters for relatively rough strips. Retaining a close family resemblance to the earlier and smaller Yak-40, the Yak-42 can take-off from airfields no larger than those required for the previously-mentioned aircraft. The first prototype (illustrated above) features 11 deg. of wing sweepback whereas the second (opposite page) has 25 deg., parallel test programmes having been conducted with these to determine the production configuration which had still to be announced at the time of closing for press. Aeroflot reportedly possesses a requirement for up to 2,000 aircraft in the Yak-42 category in the 1980–90 timescale.

212

YAKOVLEV YAK-42

Dimensions: Span, 114 ft 10 in (35,00 m); length, 114 ft 10 in (35,00 m).

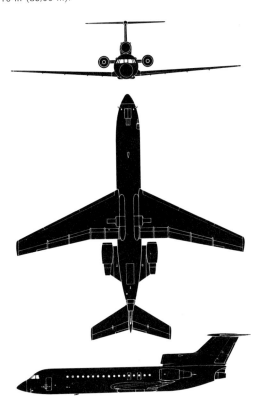

YAKOVLEV YAK-50

Country of Origin: USSR.

Type: Single-seat aerobatic competition aircraft.

Power Plant: One 360 hp Vedeneev M-14P nine-cylinder radial air-cooled engine.

Performance: Max. speed, 186 mph (300 km/h) at sea level; cruise, 155 mph (250 km/h) at sea level; initial climb rate, 3,150 ft/min (16 m/sec).

Weights: Empty, 1,552 lb (704 kg). Max. take-off, 1,320 lb (900 kg).

Status: Flown in prototype form early in 1975, with first production deliveries commencing early 1976.

Notes: While possessing a close family resemblance to the aerobatic versions of the Yak-18 (e.g., Yak-18PM and PS), the Yak-50 is an entirely new design and is of all-metal construction whereas its predecessors were of mixed construction. Flying the Yak-50, the Soviet aerobatic team made a clean sweep of the Eighth World Aerobatic Championships held in Kiev, Ukraine, during August 1976, winning the team prize and the individual male and female championships. Built by Yakovlev's Arseniyev factory in the Far East, the Yak-50 is being manufactured in limited quantities for the schools and flying clubs of the DOSAAF (Volunteer Society for Co-operation with the Army, Aviation and the Fleet) organisation, and development of a two-seat version has been reported.

YAKOVLEV YAK-50

Dimensions: Span, 31 ft 2 in (9.50 m); length, 24 ft 5½ in (7,62 m); wing area, 161·5 sq ft (15,00 m²).

ZLIN 50L

Country of Origin: Czechoslovakia.
Type: Single-seat aerobatic competition aircraft.
Power Plant: One 260 hp Avco Lycoming AEIO-540-D4B5 six-cylinder horizontally-opposed engine.
Performance: Max. speed, 177 mph (285 km/h); max. continuous cruise, 158 mph (255 km/h); range, 155 mls (255 km), with 11 Imp gal (50 l) wingtip tanks, 466 mls (750 km); initial climb, 2,953 ft/min (15,0 m/sec).
Weights: Empty, 1,257 lb (570 kg), ferrying condition, 1,279 lb (580 kg); max. take-off, 1,587 lb (720 kg), ferrying condition, 1,764 lb (800 kg).
Status: First prototype flown July 1, 1975, with second prototype and first pre-production examples following in 1976.
Notes: Intended primarily for international aerobatic competition flying, the Z 50L is expected to be produced in two versions; an aerobatic single-seater (illustrated and described) and a single-seat tourer. The Z 50L participated in the Eighth World Aerobatic Championships held at Kiev in August 1976, and makes interesting comparison with the Cranfield A1 (pages 56–57), the Mudry CAP 20L (pages 156–57) and the Yak-50 (pages 214–15). The Z 50L is of all-metal construction with aluminium-clad duralumin sheet skinning, has leaf spring steel legs and a one-piece blown cockpit canopy which may be jettisoned in an emergency. A pair of 11 Imp gal (50 l) wingtip auxiliary fuel tanks may be fitted for ferrying purposes and these are intended to be standard for the proposed touring model.

ZLIN 50L

Dimensions: Span, 28 ft 1¾ in (8,58 m); length, 21 ft 8½ in (6,62 m); height, 6 ft 1⅕ in (1,86 m); wing area, 134·55 sq ft (12,50 m²).

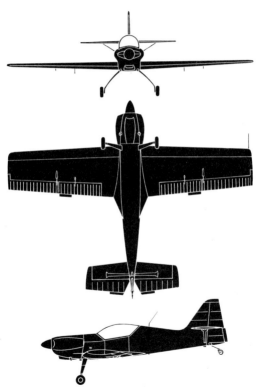

AÉROSPATIALE SA 319B ALOUETTE III

Country of Origin: France.
Type: Light utility helicopter (seven seats).
Power Plant: One 789 shp Turboméca Astazou XIVH turbo-shaft.
Performance: Max. speed, 137 mph (220 km/h) at sea level; max. cruise, 122 mph (197 km/h); max. inclined climb, 885 ft/min (4,49 m/sec); hovering ceiling (in ground effect), 10,170 ft (3 100 m), (out of ground effect), 5,575 ft (1 700 m); range (six passengers), 375 mls (605 km).
Weights: Empty, 2,442 lb (1 108 kg); max. take-off, 4,960 lb (2 250 kg).
Dimensions: Rotor diam, 36 ft 1¾ in (11,02 m); fuselage length, 32 ft 10¾ in (10,03 m).
Notes: The SA 319B is an Astazou-powered derivative of the Artouste-powered SA 316B Alouette III. All Alouette IIIs built prior to 1970 had the Artouste turboshaft, and more than 1,300 Alouette IIIs (all versions) had been ordered by 71 countries by the beginning of 1977. Licence production has been undertaken in India, Romania and Switzerland. The naval version (illustrated) fulfils a variety of shipborne roles and for the ASW task may be fitted with search radar, MAD (Magnetic Anomaly Detection) equipment and two Mk 44 homing torpedoes. The SA 319B may also be fitted with a gyro-stabilised sight and two wire-guided AS.12 or four AS.11 missiles for the anti-armour role.

AÉROSPATIALE SA 330J PUMA

Country of Origin: France.
Type: Medium transport helicopter.
Power Plant: Two 1,575 shp Turboméca IVC turboshafts.
Performance: Max. speed, 163 mph (262 km/h); max. continuous cruise at sea level, 159 mph (257 km/h); max. inclined climb, 1,400 ft/min (7,1 m/sec); hovering ceiling (in ground effect), 7,315 ft (2 230 m), (out of ground effect), 4,430 ft (1 350 m); max. range (standard fuel), 342 mls (550 km).
Weights: Operational empty, 10,060 lb (4 563 kg); max. take-off, 16,315 lb (7 400 kg).
Dimensions: Rotor diam, 49 ft 2½ in (15,00 m); fuselage length, 46 ft 1½ in (14,06 m).
Notes: The civil SA 330J and the equivalent military SA 330K were the current production models of the Puma at the beginning of 1977 when more than 470 Pumas of all versions had been ordered. The SA 330J and 330K differ from the civil SA 330F (passenger) and 330G (cargo), and SA 330H (military) models that immediately preceded them in having new plastic blades accompanied by increases in gross weights. The SA 330B (French Army), SA 330C (export) and SA 330E (RAF) had 1,328 shp Turmo IIIC4 turboshafts. The SA 330Z is a test vehicle for the currently projected SA 331 Super Puma with 1,800 shp Turboméca Makila turboshafts and a stretched fuselage to accommodate up to 26 persons. Components for the Puma are supplied by Westland in the UK.

AÉROSPATIALE SA 342 GAZELLE

Country of Origin: France.
Type: Five-seat light utility helicopter.
Power Plant: One 870 shp Turboméca Astazou XIVH turboshaft.
Performance: Max. speed, 193 mph (310 km/h); max. continuous cruise at sea level, 168 mph (270 km/h); max. inclined climb, 2,066 ft/min (10,5 m/sec); hovering ceiling (in ground effect), 13,120 ft (4 000 m), (out of ground effect), 10,330 ft (3 150 m); range at sea level, 488 mls (785 km).
Weights: Empty equipped, 2,114 lb (959 kg); max. take-off, 4,190 lb (1 900 kg).
Dimensions: Rotor diam, 34 ft 5½ in (10,50 m); fuselage length, 31 ft 2¾ in (9,53 m).
Notes: The SA 342 is a more powerful derivative of the SA 341 (592 shp Astazou IIIA) and has been exported to Kuwait, Iraq and elsewhere, and is equipped to launch four HOT missiles, AS-11s or other weapons. A civil equivalent, the SA 342J offering a 220 lb (100 kg) increase in payload, will be available in 1977, production of the SA 341 and 342 Gazelles averaging 15 monthly at the beginning of that year. Versions of the lower-powered SA 341 comprise the SA 341B (British Army), SA 341C (British Navy), SA 341D (RAF), SA 341F (French Army), SA 341G (civil version) and SA 341H (military export version). Sub-assemblies are supplied by Westland, final assembly being by Aérospatiale.

220

AÉROSPATIALE AS 350B ECUREUIL

Country of Origin: France.

Type: Light general-purpose utility helicopter.

Power Plant: One 740 shp Turboméca Arriel or 592 shp Avco Lycoming LTS 101 turboshaft.

Performance: (Arriel turboshaft) Max. speed, 166 mph (267 km/h); max. continuous cruise at sea level, 143 mph (230 km/h); hovering ceiling (in ground effect), 10,660 ft (3 250 m), (out of ground effect), 8,200 ft (2 500 m); range, 430 mls (690 km).

Weights: Empty equipped, 2,094 lb (950 kg); max. take-off, 4,630 lb (2 100 kg).

Dimensions: Rotor diam, 35 ft 0¾ in (10,69 m); fuselage length, 35 ft 9½ in (10,91 m).

Notes: First (LTS 101-powered) Ecureuil (Squirrel) prototype flown on June 27, 1974, with second (Arriel-powered) following in February 1975. The Ecureuil is being offered with both the above-mentioned turboshafts and the first production examples (both LTS 101- and Arriel-powered) were completed late in 1976 with the first customer deliveries scheduled for the second half of 1977. The standard production model is a six-seater and features include a Starflex all-plastic rotor head, simplified dynamic machinery and modular assemblies to simplify changes in the field. Twin-engined versions are being actively considered.

AÉROSPATIALE SA 360C DAUPHIN

Country of Origin: France.

Type: Multi-purpose and transport helicopter.

Power Plant: One 1,035 shp (derated to 873 shp) Turboméca Astazou XVIIA turboshaft.

Performance: Max. speed, 196 mph (315 km/h); max. continuous cruise at sea level, 168 mph (270 km/h; max. inclined climb rate, 1,968 ft/min (10,0 m/sec); hovering ceiling at 5,732 lb/2,600 kg (in ground effect), 10,750 ft (3 275 m), (out of ground effect), 8,700 ft (2 650 m); range (at 6,614 lb/3 000 kg), 407 mls (655 km).

Weights: Empty equipped, 3,540 lb (1 606 kg); max. take-off, 6,614 lb (3 000 kg).

Dimensions: Rotor diam, 37 ft 8¾ in (11,50 m); fuselage length, 36 ft 4 in (10,98 m).

Notes: The Dauphin is intended for both civil and military roles and two prototypes made their initial flights on June 2, 1972 and January 29, 1973 respectively, production deliveries being initiated in 1976. The SA 360C may be fitted with a gyro-stabilised weapons aiming sight and eight HOT (High-subsonic Optically-guided Tube-launched) missiles for the anti-armour role and the single-engined Dauphin will accommodate up to 10 persons in the transport role. An experimental variant with a derated 1,280 shp Astazou XX turboshaft, the SA 361, entered its test programme during the course of 1976.

AÉROSPATIALE SA 365 DAUPHIN 2

Country of Origin: France.
Type: Multi-purpose and transport helicopter.
Power Plant: Two 680 shp Turboméca Arriel turboshafts.
Performance: Max. speed, 196 mph (315 km/h); max. continuous cruise at sea level, 163 mph (262 km/h); max. inclined climb rate, 1,653 ft/min (8,4 m/s); hovering ceiling (both in and out of ground effect), 15,000 ft (4 575 m); range, 339 mls (545 km).
Weights: Empty equipped, 3,980 lb (1 806 kg); max. take-off, 7,495 lb (3 400 kg).
Dimensions: Main rotor diam, 37 ft 8¾ in (11,50 m); fuselage length, 36 ft 3⅞ in (10,98 m).
Notes: First flown on January 24, 1975, with production deliveries scheduled for mid-1977, the SA 365 Dauphin 2 can accommodate up to 14 persons. Fitted with an all-plastic Starflex rotor head, the Dauphin 2 is offered for both civil and military roles, a proposed naval version having a nosewheel undercarriage, nose-mounted search radar, a gyro-stabilised weapons aiming sight, MAD (Magnetic Anomaly Detection) equipment and radio-command AS-15 anti-shipping missiles. A variant of the Dauphin 2, the SA 366 powered by two Avco Lycoming LTS101 turboshafts, was tested in prototype form but subsequently shelved and consideration is being given to a development of the helicopter with two uprated (730 shp) Arriel turboshafts.

AGUSTA A 109 HIRUNDO

Country of Origin: Italy.
Type: Eight-seat light utility helicopter.
Power Plant: Two 420 shp Allison 250-C20B turboshafts.
Performance: (At 5,402 lb/2 450 kg) Max. speed, 192 mph (310 km/h); max. continuous cruise, 173 mph (278 km/h) at sea level; hovering ceiling (in ground effect), 9,800 ft (2 987 m), (out of ground effect), 6,700 ft (2 042 m); max. inclined climb, 1,600 ft/min (8,12 m/sec); max. range, 385 mls (620 km) at 148 mph (238 km/h).
Weights: Empty equipped, 2,998 lb (1 360 kg); max. take-off, 5,402 lb (2 450 kg).
Dimensions: Rotor diam, 36 ft 1 in (11,00 m); fuselage length, 36 ft 10$\frac{7}{8}$ in (11,25 m).
Notes: The first of four Hirundo (Swallow) prototypes flew on August 4, 1971. A pre-production batch of 10 Hirundos was followed by first customer deliveries late 1976, and production tempo had attained six per month by the beginning of 1977, with a planned rate of 20 per month by the end of the year. The Hirundo is currently being offered for both civil and military roles, five having been delivered to the Italian Army, including two equipped to launch TOW (Tube-launched Optically-tracked Wire-guided) missiles. Proposed variants include a naval Hirundo with search radar, gyro-stabilised weapons aiming sight and torpedo or rocket armament, and the A 129 will be an attack derivative.

AGUSTA-BELL AB 212ASW

Country of Origin: Italy.

Type: Anti-submarine and anti-surface vessel helicopter.

Power Plant: One 1,290 shp (derated from 1,875 shp) Pratt & Whitney PT6T-6 coupled turboshaft.

Performance: (At 11,197 lb/5 080 kg) Max. speed, 122 mph (196 km/h) at sea level; max. cruise, 115 mph (185 km/h); max. inclined climb, 1,450 ft/min (7,38 m/sec); hovering ceiling (in ground effect), 12,500 ft (3 810 m), (out of ground effect), 4,000 ft (1,220 m); range (15% reserves), 414 mls (667 km) at sea level.

Weights: Empty equipped, 7,540 lb (3 420 kg); max. take-off, 11,197 lb (5 080 kg).

Dimensions: Rotor diam, 48 ft 2½ in (14,69 m); fuselage length, 42 ft 10¾ in (13,07 m).

Notes: The AB 212ASW is an Italian anti-submarine derivative of the Bell 212 Twin Two-Twelve (see page 230) developed primarily for use by the Italian Navy (to which 28 examples are being delivered) and for export (batches having been delivered to Spain and Turkey). For the ASW mission, the AB 212ASW carries high-performance long-range search radar, ECM equipment, a gyro-stabilised sighting system and a pair of Mk 44 or Mk 46 homing torpedoes or depth charges. Agusta also manufactures the standard AB 212 and the AB 205 Iroquois (see page 226), combined production rate being 12–15 monthly at the beginning of 1977.

BELL MODEL 205A-1 (IROQUOIS)

Country of Origin: USA.

Type: Fifteen-seat utility helicopter.

Power Plant: One 1,400 shp Lycoming T5313A turboshaft.

Performance: (At 9,500 lb/4 309 kg) Max. speed, 127 mph (204 km/h) at sea level; max. cruise, 111 mph (179 km/h) at 8,000 ft (2 440 m); max. inclined climb, 1,680 ft/min (8,53 m/sec); hovering ceiling (in ground effect), 10,400 ft (3 170 m), (out of ground effect), 6,000 ft (1 830 m); range, 344 mls (553 km) at 8,000 ft (2 440 m).

Weights: Empty equipped, 5,082 lb (2 305 kg); normal take-off, 9,500 lb (4 309 kg).

Dimensions: Rotor diam, 48 ft 0 in (14,63 m); fuselage length, 41 ft 6 in (12,65 m).

Notes: The Model 205A is basically similar to the Model 204B (see 1973 edition) but introduces a longer fuselage with increased cabin space. It is produced under licence in Italy by Agusta as the AB 205, and is assembled under licence in Formosa (Taiwan). The initial version for the US Army, the UH-1D, had a 1,100 shp T53-L-11 turboshaft. This model was manufactured under licence in Federal Germany. The UH-1D has been succeeded in production for the US Army by the UH-1H with a 1,400 shp T53-L-13 turboshaft, and a similar helicopter for the Mobile Command of the Canadian Armed Forces is designated CUH-1H. A progressive development is the Model 214 (see page 231).

BELL MODEL 206B JETRANGER II

Country of Origin: USA.
Type: Five-seat light utility helicopter.
Power Plant: One 400 shp Allison 250-C20 turboshaft.
Performance: (At 3,000 lb/1 361 kg) Max. cruise, 136 mph (219 km/h) at sea level, 142 mph (228 km/h) at 5,000 ft (1 524 m); hovering ceiling (in ground effect), 13,200 ft (4 023 m), (out of ground effect), 8,700 ft (2 652 m); max. inclined climb, 1,540 ft/min (7,82 m/sec); max. range, 436 mls (702 km) at 10,000 ft (3 048 m).
Weights: Empty, 1,455 lb (660 kg); max. take-off, 3,000 lb (1 360 kg).
Dimensions: Rotor diam, 33 ft 4 in (10,16 m); fuselage length, 31 ft 2 in (9,50 m).
Notes: The JetRanger is manufactured in both commercial and military versions, and the current production variant, the Model 206B JetRanger II, differs from the Model 206A Jet-Ranger in having an uprated turboshaft. A light observation version for the US Army is known as the OH-58A Kiowa, and a training version for the US Navy is known as the TH-57A SeaRanger. An Australian-built version of the Model 206B has been delivered to the Australian Army, and this helicopter is also built in Italy by Agusta as the AB 206B-1. The OH-58A Kiowa has a larger main rotor of 35 ft 4 in (10,77 m) diameter and a fuselage of 32 ft 3½ in (9,84 m) length.

227

BELL MODEL 206L LONG RANGER

Country of Origin: USA.

Type: Seven-seat light utility helicopter.

Power Plant: One 420 shp Allison 250-C20B turboshaft.

Performance: (At 3,900 lb/1 769 kg) Max. speed, 144 mph (232 km/h); cruise, 136 mph (229 km/h) at sea level; hovering ceiling (in ground effect), 8,200 ft (2 499 m), (out of ground effect), 2,000 ft (610 m); range, 390 mls (628 km) at sea level, 430 mls (692 km) at 5,000 ft (1 524 m).

Weights: Empty, 1,861 lb (844 kg); max. take-off, 4,000 lb (1 814 kg).

Dimensions: Rotor diam. 37 ft 0 in (11,28 m); fuselage length, 33 ft 3 in (10,13 m).

Notes: The Model 206L Long Ranger is a stretched and more powerful version of the Model 206B JetRanger II, with a longer fuselage, increased fuel capacity, an uprated engine and a larger rotor. The Long Ranger is being manufactured in parallel with the JetRanger II and initial customer deliveries commenced late in 1975, prototype testing having been initiated during the course of 1973. The Long Ranger is available with emergency flotation gear and with a 2,000-lb (907-kg) capacity cargo hook. Cabin volume is 83 cu ft (2,35 m³) as compared with the 49 cu ft (1,39 m³) of the JetRanger II (see page 225). By 1977, some 5,000 commercial and military examples of the basic JetRanger series had been delivered. Licence manufacture is undertaken in Italy by Agusta.

BELL MODEL 209 HUEYCOBRA

Country of Origin: USA.

Type: Two-seat attack helicopter.

Power Plant: One (AH-1J) 1,800 shp Pratt & Whitney (Canada) T400-CP-400 or (AH-1T) 1,970 shp T400-WV-402 coupled turboshaft.

Performance: (AH-1J at 10,000 lb/4 535 kg) Max. speed, 207 mph (333 km/h) at sea level; max. inclined climb, 1,090 ft/min (5,54 m/sec); hovering ceiling (in ground effect), 12,450 ft (3 794 m); max. range (without reserves), 359 mls (577 km).

Weights: Empty equipped (AH-1J), 6,816 lb (3 091 kg), (AH-1T) 8,489 lb (3 854 kg); max. take-off (AH-1J), 10,000 lb (4 535 kg), (AH-1T), 14,000 lb (6 356 kg).

Dimensions: Rotor diam (AH-1J), 44 ft 0 in (13,41 m), (AH-1T) 48 ft 0 in (14,64 m); fuselage length, 44 ft 7 in (13,59 m).

Notes: The twin-engined (coupled turboshaft) version of the Model 209 is being produced in two versions, the first of these, the AH-1J, being essentially a "Twin Pac" powered version of the US Marine Corps' AH-1G SeaCobra (1,100 shp Lycoming T53-L-13), and in addition to being supplied to the USMC, this model is being manufactured for Iran (202 examples). The AH-1T (illustrated) flew in 1976 and differs in having the dynamic components of the Model 214 (see page 231), and 10 are on order for the USMC.

BELL MODEL 212 TWIN TWO-TWELVE

Country of Origin: USA.

Type: Fifteen-seat utility helicopter.

Power Plant: One 1,800 shp Pratt & Whitney PT6T-3 coupled turboshaft.

Performance: Max. speed, 121 mph (194 km/h) at sea level; max. inclined climb at 10,000 lb (4 535 kg), 1,460 ft/min (7,4 m/sec); hovering ceiling (in ground effect), 17,100 ft (5 212 m), (out of ground effect), 9,900 ft (3 020 m); max. range, 296 mls (476 km) at sea level.

Weights: Empty, 5,500 lb (2 495 kg); max. take-off, 10,000 lb (4 535 kg).

Dimensions: Rotor diam, 48 ft 2½ in (14,69 m); fuselage length, 42 ft 10¾ in (13,07 m).

Notes: The Model 212 is based on the Model 205 (see page 226) from which it differs primarily in having a twin-engined power plant (two turboshaft engines coupled to a combining gearbox with a single output shaft), and both commercial and military versions are being produced. A model for the Canadian Armed Forces is designated CUH-1N, and an essentially similar variant of the Model 212, the UH-1N, is being supplied to the USAF, the USN, and the USMC. All versions of the Model 212 can carry an external load of 4,400 lb (1 814 kg), and can maintain cruise performance on one engine component at maximum gross weight.

BELL MODEL 214B

Country of Origin: USA.

Type: Sixteen-seat utility helicopter.

Power Plant: One 2,930 shp Avco Lycoming T5508D turboshaft.

Performance: Max. speed, 190 mph (305 km/h) at sea level; max. cruise (at gross weight of 13,000 lb/5 897 kg), 150 mph (241 km/h); range, 300 mls (483 km).

Weights: Normal max. take-off, 13,000 lb (5 897 kg), (with slung load), 16,000 lb (7 257 kg).

Dimensions: Rotor diam, 50 ft 0 in (15,20 m).

Notes: Development of the Model 214, originally known as the HueyPlus, was initiated in 1970 as a progressive development of the Model 205 (UH-1H). Utilising an essentially similar airframe with strengthened main beams, pylon structure and aft fuselage, and the main rotor and tail rotor drive systems of the Model 309 KingCobra (see 1973 edition) coupled with the Lycoming T55-L-7C turboshaft installed in the second KingCobra, this utility helicopter is being developed for military use as the Model 214A and was certificated in 1975 for commercial use as the Model 214B. First flight of the Model 214A took place on March 13, 1974, and first deliveries against orders from the Iranian Government for 287 helicopters of this type began in April 1975, and was continuing at 10 per month at the beginning of 1977. Four hundred additional Model 214As are to be co-produced by Bell and the Iranian government.

BELL MODEL 222

Country of Origin: USA.

Type: Light utility and transport helicopter.

Power Plant: Two 650 shp Avco Lycoming LTS 101-650C turboshafts.

Performance: Max. speed, 180 mph (290 km/h); range cruise, 160 mph (257 km/h); range (with reserves at range cruise), 420 mls (675 km).

Weights: Empty, 3,970 lb (1 800 kg); max. take-off, 6,700 lb (3 042 kg).

Dimensions: Rotor diam, 30 ft 0 in (11,89 m); fuselage length, 39 ft 9 in (12,12 m).

Notes: Designed to accommodate up to 10 persons (including pilot) in a high-density arrangement, with a standard interior providing eight seats and an executive six-seater, the Model 222 is the first US light twin-turbine helicopter and the first of three prototypes was flown on August 13, 1976, with initial production deliveries scheduled for 1978. The Model 222 may be fitted with flotation gear or fixed skids as alternatives to the retractable tricycle wheel undercarriage, and kits are being developed to suit it for use in the aeromedical role with two casualty litters and two seated casualties or medical attendants accommodated in the cabin. Particular attention has been paid in the design to the reduction of cabin noise levels.

BOEING VERTOL MODEL 114

Country of Origin: USA.

Type: Medium transport helicopter.

Power Plant: (CH-47C) Two 3,750 shp Lycoming T55-L-11 turboshafts.

Performance: (CH-47C at 33,000 lb/14 969 kg) Max. speed, 190 mph (306 km/h) at sea level; average cruise, 158 mph (254 km/h); max. inclined climb, 2,880 ft/min (14,63 m/sec); hovering ceiling (out of ground effect), 14,750 ft (4 495 m); mission radius, 115 mls (185 km).

Weights: Empty, 20,378 lb (9 243); max. take-off, 46,000 lb (20 865 kg).

Dimensions: Rotor diam (each), 60 ft 0 in (18,29 m); fuselage length, 51 ft 0 in (15,54 m).

Notes: The Model 114 is the standard medium transport helicopter of the US Army, and is operated by that service under the designation CH-47 Chinook. The initial production model, the CH-47A, was powered by 2,200 shp T55-L-5 or 2,650 shp T55-L-7 turboshafts. This was succeeded by the CH-47B with 2,850 shp T55-L-7C engines, redesigned rotor blades and other modifications, and this, in turn, gave place to the current CH-47C with more powerful engines, strengthened transmissions, and increased fuel capacity. This model is manufactured in Italy by Elicotteri Meriodionali, orders calling for 24 (of 26) for the Italian Army and 18 (of 42) for the Iranian Army.

BOEING VERTOL MODEL 179

Country of Origin: USA.
Type: Commercial transport helicopter.
Power Plant: Two 1,536 shp General Electric T700-GE-700 turboshafts.
Performance: Max. continuous cruise at sea level, 179 mph (289 km/h); range cruise at sea level, 134 mph (216 km/h); hovering ceiling (out of ground effect), 5,650 ft (1 722 m); max. range (no reserves), 599 mls (964 km).
Weights: Empty equipped, 9,400 lb (4 264 kg); max. take-off, 18,700 lb (8 481 kg).
Dimensions: Rotor diam, 49 ft 0 in (14,93 m); fuselage length, 56 ft 6 in (16,00 m).
Notes: The commercial Model 179 is a derivative of Boeing Vertol's unsuccessful contender for the US Army's UTTAS (Utility Tactical Transport Aircraft System) and a company-funded prototype commenced trials in July 1975, the first customer deliveries being scheduled for 1978 delivery. The Model 179 offers alternative seating arrangements for 19 and 14 passengers, and a company executive transport version is proposed with accommodation for six passengers. The Model 179 will have full IFR capability and the advanced technology features developed for the YUH-61A UTTAS and embodied by the commercial version will ensure high standards of reliability and safety, coupled with low noise and vibration levels

HUGHES 500D

Country of Origin: USA.
Type: Light utility helicopter.
Power Plant: One 420 shp Allison 250-C20B turboshaft.
Performance: Max. speed, 173 mph (278 km/h) at sea level; max. continuous cruise, 159 mph (255 km/h) at 5,000 ft (1 525 m); econ. cruise, 146 mph (235 km/h); max. inclined climb, 1,918 ft/min (9,66 m/sec); hovering ceiling (out of ground effect), 7,800 ft (2 375 m); max. range, 369 mls (594 km); range with max. payload, 334 mls (537 km).
Weights: Empty equipped, 1,320 lb (598 km); max. take-off, 3,000 lb (1 360 kg).
Dimensions: Rotor diam, 26 ft 5 in (8,05 m); fuselage length, 23 ft 0 in (7,01 m).
Notes: The Model 500D is a progressive development of the Model 500C with an uprated engine and a small T-tail to improve flight stability at both ends of the speed range. Deliveries of the Model 500D commenced in 1976, in which year some 50 were delivered, and production is scheduled to attain 15 per month during 1977. The military equivalent, the Model 500M-D Defender, is to be licence manufactured in the Republic of Korea, 100 having been ordered by the Republic of Korea Air Force for light observation and anti-armour roles, 34 of these being delivered by the parent company. The Model 500M-D is armed with a 7,62-mm Minigun and can carry four TOW anti-tank missiles.

HUGHES YAH-64

Country of Origin: USA.
Type: Tandem two-seat attack helicopter.
Power Plant: Two 1,536 shp General Electric T700-GE-700 turboshafts.
Performance: (Estimated) Max. speed, 191 mph (307 km/h); max. continuous cruise, 180 mph (290 km/h); max. inclined climb, 3,200 ft/min (16,25 m/sec); hovering ceiling (in ground effect), 14,600 ft (4 450 m), (out of ground effect), 11,800 ft (3 597 m); max. range (internal fuel), 359 mls (577 km); ferry range (external fuel), 1,168 mls (1 880 km).
Weights: Empty equipped, 9,500 lb (4 309 kg); max. take-off, 17,400 lb (7 892 kg).
Dimensions: Rotor diam, 48 ft 0 in (14,63 m).
Notes: The YAH-64 is one of two designs selected by the US Army for competitive evaluation in 1976 for selection as the service's AAH (Advanced Attack Helicopter), the competing design being the Bell YAH-63 (see 1976 Edition). The two prototypes of the YAH-64 were flown on September 30 and November 22, 1975, and the type was selected as the AAH in December 1976. Smaller and lighter than the YAH-63, the YAH-64 has a single-barrel 30-mm gun, which, based on the chain-driven bolt system, is suspended beneath the forward fuselage, the gunner occupying the forward cockpit. Eight BGM-71A TOW (Tube-launched Optically-tracked Wire-guided) missiles may be carried.

KAMOV KA-25 (HORMONE A)

Country of Origin: USSR.

Type: Shipboard anti-submarine warfare helicopter.

Power Plant: Two 900 shp Glushenkov GTD-3 turboshafts.

Performance: (Estimated) Max. speed, 130 mph (209 km/h); normal cruise, 120 mph (193 km/h); max. range, 400 mls (644 km); service ceiling, 11,000 ft (3 353 m).

Weights: (Estimated) Empty, 10,500 lb (4 765 kg); max. take-off, 16,500 lb (7 484 kg).

Dimensions: Rotor diam (each), 51 ft 7½ in (15,74 m); approx. fuselage length, 35 ft 6 in (10,82 m).

Notes: Possessing a basically similar airframe to that of the Ka-25K (see 1973 edition) and employing a similar self-contained assembly comprising rotors, transmission, engines and auxiliaries, the Ka-25 serves with the Soviet Navy primarily in the ASW role but is also employed in the utility and transport roles. The ASW Ka-25 serves aboard the helicopter cruisers *Moskva* and *Leningrad*, and the carrier *Kiev*, as well as with shore-based units. A search radar installation is mounted in a nose radome, but other sensor housings and antennae differ widely from helicopter to helicopter. There is no evidence that externally-mounted weapons may be carried. Each landing wheel is surrounded by an inflatable pontoon surmounted by inflation bottles. Sufficient capacity is available to accommodate up to a dozen personnel.

MBB BO 105C

Country of Origin: Federal Germany.
Type: Five/six-seat light utility helicopter.
Power Plant: Two 400 shp Allison 250-C20 turboshafts.
Performance: Max. speed, 155 mph (250 km/h) at sea level; max. cruise, 138 mph (222 km/h); max. inclined climb, 1,870 ft/min (9,5 m/sec); hovering ceiling (in ground effect), 7,610 ft (2 320 m), (out of ground effect), 5,085 ft (1 550 m); normal range, 388 mls (625 km) at 5,000 ft (1 525 m).
Weights: Empty, 2,360 lb (1 070 kg); normal take-off, 4,630 lb (2 100 kg); max. take-off, 5,070 lb (2 300 kg).
Dimensions: Rotor diam, 32 ft 1¾ in (9,80 m); fuselage length, 28 ft 0½ in (8,55 m).
Notes: The BO 105 features a rigid unarticulated main rotor with folding glass-fibre reinforced plastic blades, and the first prototype (with a conventional rotor) was tested in 1966, three prototypes being followed by four pre-production examples, and production deliveries commencing during 1971. The German Army has ordered 227 for observation and anti-armour roles. The third prototype was powered by 375 shp MTU 6022 turboshafts, but the production model has standardised on the Allison 250. Production is undertaken by the Siebelwerke-ATG subsidiary of MBB and manufacture is undertaken in Indonesia and the Philippines. The dynamic components of the BO 105 are being used for the larger BO 107.

MIL MI-8 (HIP)

Country of Origin: USSR.

Type: General-purpose transport helicopter.

Power Plant: Two 1,500 shp Isotov TV-2-117A turboshafts.

Performance: (At 24,470 lb/11 100 kg) Max. speed, 155 mph (250 km/h); max. cruise, 140 mph (225 km/h); hovering ceiling (in ground effect), 5,900 ft (1 800 m), (out of ground effect), 2,625 ft (800 m); service ceiling, 14,760 ft (4 500 m); range with 6,615 lb (3 000 kg) of freight, 264 mls (425 km).

Weights: Empty (cargo), 15,787 lb (7 171 kg), (passenger), 16,352 lb (7 417 kg); normal take-off, 24,470 lb (11 100 kg); max. take-off (for VTO), 26,455 lb (12 000 kg).

Dimensions: Rotor diam, 69 ft 10¼ in (21,29 m); fuselage length, 59 ft 7⅓ in (18,17 m).

Notes: The Mi-8 has been in continuous production since 1964 for both civil and military tasks. The standard commercial passenger version has a basic flight crew of two or three and 28 four-abreast seats, and the aeromedical version accommodates 12 casualty stretchers and a medical attendant. As a freighter the Mi-8 will carry up to 8,818 lb (4 000 kg) of cargo, and military tasks include assault transport, search and rescue, and anti-submarine warfare. The Mi-8 is now operated by several Warsaw Pact air forces, serving primarily in the support transport role, and has been exported to numerous countries, including Finland, Pakistan and Egypt.

MIL MI-24 (HIND)

Country of Origin: USSR.

Type: Gunship and assault transport helicopter.

Power Plant: Two 1,500 shp Isotov TV-2-117A turboshafts.

Performance: (Estimated) Max. speed, 160 mph (257 km/h); max. cruise, 140 mph (225 km/h); hovering ceiling (in ground effect), 6,000 ft (1 830 m), (out of ground effect), 1,600 ft (790 m); normal range, 300 mls (480 km).

Weights: Normal loaded, 25,000 lb (11 340 kg).

Dimensions: Rotor diam., 55 ft 0 in (16,76 m); fuselage length, 55 ft 6 in (16,90 m).

Notes: Employed in considerable numbers by the Soviet forces, the Mi-24 is apparently serving in two versions. One version (*Hind-A*), illustrated above, has three weapons stations on each auxiliary wing, the two inboard stations carrying UV-32-57 rocket pods and the outboard station taking the form of a vertical extension of the wingtip with a double carrier for two AT-3 *Sagger* wire-guided anti-t; missiles. The other version (*Hind-B*) does not have the w tip vertical extensions. Both versions have a 12,7 machine gun in the extreme fuselage nose, armour protec for the flight crew and accommodation for 8–12 ass troops with a large door aft of the flight deck on each si enabling them to exit rapidly. The Mi-24 may utilise some of the components of the Mi-8 (see page 239) but appears to be somewhat smaller.

SIKORSKY S-61D (SEA KING)

Country of Origin: USA.

Type: Amphibious anti-submarine helicopter.

Power Plant: Two 1,500 shp General Electric T58-GE-10 turboshafts.

Performance: Max. speed, 172 mph (277 km/h) at sea level; inclined climb, 2,200 ft/min (11,2 m/sec); hovering ceiling (out of ground effect), 8,200 ft (2 500 m); range (with 10% reserves), 622 mls (1 000 km).

Weights: Empty equipped, 12,087 lb (5 481 kg); max. take-off, 20,500 lb (9 297 kg).

Dimensions: Rotor diam, 62 ft 0 in (18,90 m); fuselage length, 54 ft 9 in (16,69 m).

Notes: A more powerful derivative of the S-61B, the S-61D serves with the US Navy as the SH-3D (illustrated above), 72 helicopters of this type following on production of 255 SH-3As (S-61Bs) for the ASW role for the US Navy, four being supplied to the Brazilian Navy and 22 to the Spanish Navy. Four similar aircraft have been supplied to the Argentine Navy as S-61D-4s and 11 have been supplied to the US Army/Marine Corps Executive Flight Detachment as VH-3Ds. Licence manufacture of the S-61D is being undertaken in the United Kingdom (see pages 247–8), in Japan for the Maritime Self-Defence Force and in Italy by Agusta for the Italian and Iranian navies. The SH-3G and SH-3H are upgraded conversions of the SH-3A.

SIKORSKY S-61R

Country of Origin: USA.

Type: Amphibious transport and rescue helicopter.

Power Plant: (CH-3E) Two 1,500 shp General Electric T58-GE-5 turboshafts.

Performance: (CH-3E at 21,247 lb/9 635 kg) Max. speed, 162 mph (261 km/h) at sea level; range cruise, 144 mph (232 km/h); max. inclined climb, 1,310 ft/min (6,6 m/sec); hovering ceiling (in ground effect), 4,100 ft (1 250 m); range with 10% reserves, 465 mls (748 km).

Weights: (CH-3E) Empty, 13,255 lb (6 010 kg); normal take-off, 21,247 lb (9 635 kg); max. take-off, 22,050 lb (10 000 kg).

Dimensions: Rotor diam, 62 ft 0 in (18,90 m); fuselage length, 57 ft 3 in (17,45 m).

Notes: Although based on the S-61A, the S-61R embodies numerous design changes, including a rear ramp and a tricycle-type undercarriage. Initial model for the USAF was the CH-3C with 1,300 shp T58-GE-1 turboshafts, but this was subsequently updated to CH-3E standards. The CH-3E can accommodate 25–30 troops or 5,000 lb (2 270 kg) of cargo, and may be fitted with a TAT-102 barbette on each sponson mounting a 7,62-mm Minigun. The HH-3E is a USAF rescue version with armour, self-sealing tanks, and refuelling probe, and the HH-3F Pelican (illustrated) is a US Coast Guard search and rescue model.

SIKORSKY S-65 (YCH-53E)

Country of Origin: USA.

Type: Amphibious assault transport helicopter.

Power Plant: Three 4,380 shp General Electric T64-GE-415 turboshafts.

Performance: Max. speed, 196 mph (315 km/h) at sea level; max. cruise, 173 mph (278 km/h).

Weights: Operational empty, 33,000 lb (14 968 kg); max. take-off, 69,750 lb (31 638 kg).

Dimensions: Rotor diam., 79 ft 0 in (24,08 m); fuselage length, 73 ft 5 in (22,38 m).

Notes: The YCH-53E is a growth version of the CH-53D Sea Stallion (see 1974 edition) embodying a third engine, an uprated transmission system, a seventh main rotor blade and increased rotor diameter. The first of two prototypes was flown on March 1, 1974, and the first of two pre-production prototypes flew on December 8, 1975, but a production decision was not anticipated prior to 1977. The YCH-53E can accommodate up to 56 troops in a high-density arrangement and can lift a 32,000-lb (14 515-kg) external load over a radius of 58 miles (93 km) at sea level in a 90 deg F temperature. The planned production programme envisages the acquisition of 70 helicopters of this type divided equally between the US Navy and US Marine Corps. The YCH-53E offers a major performance advance and can retrieve 93 per cent of USMC tactical aircraft without disassembly.

SIKORSKY S-70 (YUH-60A)

Country of Origin: USA.

Type: Tactical transport helicopter.

Power Plant: Two 1,536 shp General Electric YT700-GE-700 turboshafts.

Performance: (Estimated) Max. speed, 200 mph (322 km/h) at sea level; cruise, 184 mph (296 km/h); hovering ceiling (in ground effect), 10,000 ft (3 048 m), (out of ground effect), 5,800 ft (1 768 m); normal range, 400 mls (740 km).

Weights: Design gross, 16,500 lb (7 485 kg); max. take-off, 22,000 lb (9 979 kg).

Dimensions: Rotor diam, 53 ft 0 in (16,15 m); fuselage length, 50 ft 11½ in (15,53 m).

Notes: The YUH-64 was winner of a fly-off with the competitive Boeing Vertol YUH-61A from early 1976, to enable the US Army to select a UTTAS (Utility Tactical Transport Aircraft System). The choice of the YUH-60A was announced in December 1976, an initial contract for 15 examples of the helicopter being awarded with deliveries commencing August 1978. The first of three YUH-60As was flown on October 17, 1974, and a company-funded fourth prototype flew on May 23, 1975, this being a demonstrator for the S-78-20, a commercial version of the YUH-60A with accommodation for 20 passengers, a projected developed version being the S-78-29.

SIKORSKY S-76

Country of Origin: USA.
Type: Fourteen-seat commercial transport helicopter.
Power Plant: Two 700 shp Allison 250-C30 turboshafts.
Performance: (Estimated) Max. speed, 179 mph (288 km/h); max. cruise, 167 mph (268 km/h); econ. cruise, 145 mph (233 km/h); hovering ceiling (in ground effect), 5,100 ft (1 524 m), (out of ground effect), 1,400 ft (427 m); range (full payload with 30 min reserves), 460 mls (740 km), (eight passengers and auxiliary fuel), 690 mls (1 110 km).
Weights: Empty, 4,942 lb (2 241 kg); max. take-off, 9,700 lb (4 399 kg).
Dimensions: Rotor diam, 44 ft 0 in (13,41 m); fuselage length, 41 ft 10 in (12,75 m).
Notes: Scheduled to commence its flight test programme in May 1977, with production deliveries to commence in July 1978, the S-76 is unique among Sikorsky commercial helicopters in that conceptually it owes nothing to an existing military model. However, although aimed primarily at the commercial market, the S-76 has been designed to conform with appropriate military specifications and will satisfy a military role without major modification of airframe or dynamic system, military customers being included among contracts being negotiated at the beginning of 1977, when orders for some 100 S-76s had been placed.

SIKORSKY S-72

Country of Origin: USA.

Type: High-speed multi-purpose research helicopter.

Power Plant: Two 1,500 shp General Electric T58-GE-5 turboshafts and (compound form) two 9,275 lb (4 207 kg) General Electric TF34-GE-2 turbofans.

Performance: (Compound configuration) Max. speed, 345 mph (555 km/h).

Weights: Empty (helicopter configuration), 14,490 lb (6 572 kg), (compound configuration), 21,022 lb (9 535 kg); max. take-off (helicopter configuration), 18,400 lb (8 346 kg), (compound configuration), 26,200 lb (11 884 kg).

Dimensions: Rotor diam, 62 ft 0 in (18,90 m); fuselage length, 70 ft 7 in (21,51 m); span (fixed wing), 45 ft $1\frac{1}{8}$ in (13,75 m); wing area, 370 sq ft (34,37 m²).

Notes: The S-72, or RSRA (Rotor Systems Research Aircraft), is to be used by NASA and the US Army for the development of advanced rotor and integrated propulsions systems. The first of two examples was flown (in helicopter configuration) on October 12, 1976, and will be tested with and without fixed wings, and with and without pylon-mounted turbofans. The S-72 may also be flown with rotor removed as a pure fixed-wing aircraft. Two tail configurations (one for helicopter and the other for compound mode) are interchangeable.

WESTLAND SEA KING MK. 2

Country of Origin: United Kingdom (US licence).
Type: Anti-submarine warfare and search-and-rescue helicopter.
Power Plant: Two 1,500 shp Rolls-Royce Gnome 1400-1 turboshafts.
Performance: Max. speed, 143 mph (230 km/h); max. continuous cruise at sea level, 131 mph (211 km/h); hovering ceiling (in ground effect), 5,000 ft (1 525 m), (out of ground effect), 3,200 ft (975 m); range (standard fuel), 764 mls (1 230 km), (auxiliary fuel), 937 mls (1 507 km).
Weights: Empty equipped (ASW), 13,672 lb (6 201 kg), (SAR), 12,376 lb (5 613 kg); max. take-off, 21,000 lb (9 525 kg).
Dimensions: Rotor diam, 62 ft 0 in (18,90 m); fuselage length, 55 ft 9¾ in (17,01 m).
Notes: The Sea King Mk 2 is an uprated version of the basic ASW and SAR derivative of the licence-built S-61D (see page 241), the first Mk 2 being flown on June 30, 1974 and being one of 10 Sea King Mk 50s ordered by the Australian Navy. Twenty-one have been ordered for the Royal Navy as Sea King HAS Mk 2s and 15 examples of a SAR version have been ordered by the RAF as Sea King HAR Mk 3s, these being scheduled to enter service during the first quarter of 1978. A total of 179 Westland-built derivatives of the S-61D (including Commandos—see page 249) had been ordered by the beginning of 1977.

WESTLAND COMMANDO MK. 2

Country of Origin: United Kingdom (US licence).
Type: Tactical transport helicopter.
Power Plant: Two 1,590 shp Rolls-Royce Gnome 1400-1 turboshafts.
Performance: Max. speed (at 19,900 lb/9 046 kg), 138 mph (222 km/h); max. cruise, 127 mph (204 km/h); max. inclined climb, 1,930 ft/min (9,8 m/sec); range (with 30 troops), 161 mls (259 km); ferry range, 1,036 mls (1 668 km).
Weights: Empty equipped, 11,487–12,122 lb (5 221–5 510 kg); max. take-off, 20,000 lb (9 072 kg).
Dimensions: Rotor diam., 62 ft 0 in (18,89 m); fuselage length, 54 ft 9 in (16,69 m).
Notes: The Commando is a Westland-developed land-based army support helicopter derivative of the licence-built Sikorsky S-61D Sea King (see page 247), search radar and other specialised items being deleted together with the sponsons which endow the Sea King with amphibious capability. The first five examples completed as Commando Mk. 1s were minimum change conversions of Sea King airframes, the first of these flying on September 12, 1973, but subsequent Commandos are being built to Mk. 2 standards with the uprated Gnome turboshafts selected for the Sea King Mk. 50s ordered by Australia. The first production deliveries (to Egypt) commenced in 1975, that illustrated having been supplied to Qatar.

WESTLAND WG.13 LYNX

Country of Origin: United Kingdom.

Type: Multi-purpose, ASW and transport helicopter.

Power Plant: Two 900 shp Rolls-Royce BS.360-07-26 Gem 100 turboshafts.

Performance: Max. speed, 207 mph (333 km/h); max. continuous sea level cruise, 170 mph (273 km/h); max. inclined climb, 1,174 ft/min (11,05 m/sec); hovering ceiling (out of ground effect), 12,000 ft (3 660 m); max. range (internal fuel), 391 mls (629 km); max. ferry range (auxiliary fuel), 787 mls (1 266 km).

Weights: (HAS Mk 2) Operational empty, 6,767–6,999 lb (3 069–3 174 kg); max. take-off, 9,500 lb (4 309 kg).

Dimensions: Rotor diam, 42 ft 0 in (12,80 m); fuselage length, 39 ft 1¼ in (11,92 m).

Notes: The first of 13 development Lynxes was flown on March 21, 1971, with the first production example (an HAS Mk 2) flying on February 10, 1976. By the beginning of 1977, when some 15 had been completed, production rate was four per month and 149 were on order, including 26 for the French Navy, 30 for the Royal Navy, 63 for the British Army, nine for the Brazilian Navy and eight (plus eight on option) for the Netherlands Navy. Production tempo is expected to attain 11 monthly in 1978. The Lynx AH Mk 1 is the British Army's general utility version and the Lynx HAS Mk 2 is the ASW version for the Royal Navy.

ACKNOWLEDGEMENTS

The author wishes to record his thanks to the following sources of copyright photographs appearing in this volume: Air Portraits, page 112; Aviation Magazine International, page 212; Flug Revue, pages 150, 152 and 188; Takeaki Hoshina, page 154; Stephen Peltz, pages 56, 142 and 221; Hans Redemann, page 14; Prof. Johannes Zopp, page 208. The three-view silhouettes published in this volume are copyright Pilot Press Limited and may not be reproduced without prior permission.

INDEX OF AIRCRAFT TYPES